D0027411

I've known Jeremy Pearsons for many years, and I love the man of God he has become. That's one reason I loved reading this book—it so clearly reflects Jeremy's passion and hunger to know God better! Jeremy has a fresh and authentic way of sharing his thought-provoking insights about who God is and what His voice sounds like—and why gaining this knowledge should matter so much to us. Jeremy says it this way: "God wants us to know Him. He is a mystery hidden *for* us. Not *from* us." I like that. It answers a yearning deep in my own heart to know the Lord more and more. This book helps us take a giant step forward in our journey toward a deeper understanding of Jesus and our true identity in Him. There is nothing more important than that.

—Rick Renner
Pastor, Teacher, Author

JEREMY**PEARSONS**
FOREWORD BY JOHN BEVERE

LEGACY
Creative Group

Unless otherwise noted, all scripture is from the *New King James Version* of the Bible © 1982 by Thomas Nelson Inc. Used by permission. All rights reserved.

Scripture quotations marked AMP are from *The Amplified Bible, Old Testament* © 1965, 1987 by The Zondervan Corporation. *The Amplified New Testament* © 1958, 1987 by The Lockman Foundation. Used by permission.

Scripture quotations marked NIV are from *The Holy Bible, New International Version* © 1973, 1978, 1984 by the International Bible Society. Used by permission of Zondervan Publishing House.

Scripture quotations marked NLT are from the *Holy Bible, New Living Translation* © 1996, 2004 by Tyndale Charitable Trust. Used by permission of Tyndale House Publishers.

Scripture quotations marked *Wuest Translation* are from *The New Testament: An Expanded Translation* by Kenneth S. Wuest © Wm. B. Eerdmans Publishing Co. 1961. All rights reserved.

Hello. My Name Is God.

ISBN 978-1-60463-017-6   30-0818

14 13 12 11 10 09   7 6 5 4 3 2

2nd Printing

© 2009 Eagle Mountain International Church Inc. aka Legacy Creative Group

Legacy Creative Group
Fort Worth, TX 76192-0001
www.hellomynameisgod.com

Printed in the United States of America. All rights reserved under International Copyright Law. No part of this book may be reproduced or transmitted in any form or by any means, electronic or mechanical, including photocopying, recording, or by any information storage and retrieval system, without the written permission of the publisher.

This book is dedicated to my wife, Sarah.

*God has been so kind and merciful to me—
and you, my love, are the proof. I love you.*

Thank you to all who contributed to and made this book possible:

John Mason, Joshua D. Lease, Sarah Pearsons,
Michael Howell, John Copeland, James Tito and
the Publications team at Kenneth Copeland Ministries

I deeply appreciate your hard work, time, and energy.
We are getting the Word out!

Table of Contents

SECTION V: YOUR HEALER

SECTION VI: HELP WANTED

SECTION VII: JESUS IS

Foreword

One of the greatest invitations and promises of all time is found in James 4:8: "Draw near to God and He will draw near to you." Many people in this current generation have grown up with a mind-set of a God who is there, but who isn't really concerned or is too busy to have a day-to-day, vibrant relationship with them. I believe this is why so many Christians are struggling with sin issues and living defeated, "just gotta get into heaven" lives. If we would only realize the great power contained within that simple invitation, we would see a generation rise up in victory.

Notice in James it doesn't say that if we draw near to God, He *might* draw near to us. I find many people approach God in their prayer times with a mentality of tossing prayers up to God for a constant thirty minutes, saying "Amen" and going on with their day. Sometimes we say so much while God is waiting to get a word in, but before He can speak we shut off our ears when we say "Amen." I remember one time when I was driving down the road, the Holy Spirit spoke to me to pull over. I pulled off the road and immediately heard the Spirit of God whisper to my heart, *Did I not say to you, "pray without ceasing"?*

I responded, "Yes, Lord, You did."

He probed further, *Is prayer a monologue or dialogue?*

I responded, "It's a dialogue, Lord, a two-way conversation."

His words came quickly: *Well, if I said to pray without ceasing, and prayer is a dialogue, then that means I am willing to communicate with you without ceasing!*

This absolutely changed the way I approached a relationship with God. Imagine that you have a friend who invites you to come over to his house for dinner. You arrive and your friend proceeds to talk to you constantly for thirty minutes. Then he takes a breath and says, "Well, it's been great spending time with you! See you next week!" Would you continue to go over to his house every week? No way! The relationship wouldn't work because it is only one-way.

God has a great desire to reveal Himself to us and build an authentic relationship with us, but the responsibility rests upon us to interact and allow Him to reveal His heart, desires, plans, and thoughts to us. I believe that my friend Jeremy Pearsons has laid out a strategic way that you can truly know God. Not a way to engage in routine memorization of the details of God, but a way to enjoy a vibrant, living relationship with the One who put the stars in the sky and called every one of them by name, and who also knows the number of hairs on your head. Prepare yourself as you journey into this book to move from knowing *who* God is to truly knowing God.

John Bevere
Author/Speaker
Messenger International
Colorado Springs/Australia/United Kingdom

SECTION I

GOD IS _____.

Chapter One

GOD IS _____.

What's in a name?

Launching into a study of all the names of God is utterly fascinating. One right after the other, each Hebrew name reveals God in new and exciting ways.

This book is not about that.

Sorry.

Instead, let me tell you about something that started with an experiment I conducted on a group of teenagers once. I told them I was going to say a name. A first name only. And they had to tell me what they thought when I said that name. Feel free to play along.

"Ready?" I said. "Tiger."

All at once, as though it had been rehearsed and there was a conductor standing before them ready to strike the downbeat, they replied in choir-like unison, "Woods!"

"OK," I said. "What else comes to mind?"

"Golfer!" some shouted.

"Just *a* golfer?" I asked.

"The *best!*" they said. "The best ever!"

This went on for just a minute or so. In that very short amount of time, we had come up with a pretty comprehensive description of Tiger Woods based solely on what comes to mind when you hear his first name.

There are some people walking around out there with some interesting first names. They mostly belong to the children of our modern celebrities. (Frank Zappa's child Moon Unit still has to be one of my favorites.)

And while it seems as though some people are willing to call their children just about anything, you will notice that there are a few names that most will stay away from. For example, you really don't hear of many kids named "Adolph" these days. Why is that? It's just like any other name in that it is a collection of vowels and consonants that get put together in a row, and *voilà*…a name.

So why no "Adolphs"? Because of the evil reputation of hatred, bigotry, murder, and destruction behind that name. I'm also guessing there has been a sharp decline over the last several years in children named "Osama."

In the same way, many parents will name their children after a beloved grandparent, aunt, or uncle. Perhaps it's because of fond memories they had with that loved one, or because of the way they impacted them positively.

My sister's name is Aubrey. Aubrey Wayne Copeland was our great-grandfather, who was loved immensely not only by us, but also by practically everyone who ever knew him. He was a giant of a man who loved God and family and wouldn't tell a lie to save his own life. A man worth naming someone after. This book is about the reputation *behind the name.*

I asked that same group of teenagers what they thought when I said the name "Jesus." Some began to list the many miracles;

others talked about the cross, the grave, resurrection, and so forth.

This response makes sense coming from a group of kids in church. That's all the stuff you're supposed to say. But what about His reputation outside the church?

Jesus once asked His disciples, "Who do men say that I am?" Their list was different than the one the teenagers gave me. They said, "Some say you are John the Baptist, some say Elijah, others Jeremiah, or one of the prophets." Then Jesus looked at them and asked, "Who do *you* say that I am?" (Matthew 16:13-15). Their answer was astounding, and we will get into that in later chapters.

But the truth is, that is still His question to us today—who do you say that I am?

There is one major flaw in my Tiger Woods experiment. Our list of characteristics was comprised solely of things we have heard *about* Tiger. We were just yelling out things we had seen on TV, read about online, or what we had heard others say he was. I didn't know him personally, and neither did anyone else in that room.

Sure, he is a great golfer, but what goes through his head when he is not on the course? What makes him happy? What makes him worry? Where does his deepest motivation and drive come from? No one would say, "I know Tiger Woods" just because he saw him on TV or read about him somewhere. And do you think that he would ever allow me or one of those teenagers to stand and speak for him at a press conference or in a lawyer's office? No! Why? Because he doesn't know me, and I don't know him.

I wonder how God feels when people claim to know Him based on things they have seen on TV, read about online, or—worse yet—heard someone else say about Him.

Fill in this blank: God is _____.

This book is about that blank. It's about how you fill it in.

It's not about how other people have filled it in. It's not about how traditional thinking has filled it in.

It's about filling it in with what we *know* to be true because it's what God has said about Himself. He put everything we can understand in the pages of an autobiography, a book full of stories that give us finite human beings a taste of His character and nature.

Throughout this book, we are going to fill that blank with what God has said He is in the pages of the Bible. At the end of this book, you will still be the one responsible for filling in that blank for yourself. I can't fill it in for you.

Who do *you* say that He is?

This book is also about answering a deceptively simple question: Would you know Him if you saw Him?

Those of us who have been involved with the Church for a long time perhaps think we know the answer beyond doubt, but I don't think the answer to that question is as straightforward as we'd like to think.

Put bluntly, like the Pharisees of Jesus' day, many people think they know what God looks like, think they know what to expect. But all too often, they're missing God's work in their lives because they have not learned to recognize His voice, don't know His purposes, and are unfamiliar with His will and His ways.

They're looking for the obvious, the scintillating, and the sensational from God—they're looking for a sign, like Him showing up in their lives blatantly as though wearing a name tag. They're unprepared for how He speaks all too often in our lives: with a still, small voice.

•••

HELLO. MY NAME IS GOD.
DO YOU WANT TO GET TO KNOW ME?

•••

What if God isn't wearing a name tag? Will you know Him?

How you fill in that blank pertains directly to how you see Him and whether or not you see His movement in your life. He's provided an introduction to Himself in the form of the Bible, and He has left a Helper with us so that we're not just left reading *about* Him.

He introduces Himself to us with an open hand of love and mercy and an offer of relationship:

"Hello. My name is God. Do you want to get to know Me?"

If so, keep reading...

Chapter Two

THE WOMAN AT THE WELL, THE COWBOY AT THE AIRPORT

Every once in a while, with little or no warning, life hands us some pretty awkward moments. One of my least favorite of them all is when I meet someone who seems to know me really well, but I can't for the life of me think of this person's name.

You know what I'm talking about and how those conversations go: "Hey, *you*. Good to see *you,* man." And a two-minute conversation ensues that can feel like an eternity.

I haven't yet decided which is worse, though: running into someone I am supposed to know in person, or answering the phone only to hear from the other end, "Hey. It's me."

Silence, followed by my uncertain reply, "Hey, *you*. Good to hear from *you.*"

Why don't I just say, "I'm sorry, who is this?" I don't know. I don't want to hurt anyone's feelings, and because of that, I make a split-second decision to let this conversation continue for as long as is necessary for me to figure out who in the world is calling me.

My brother-in-law once received a Happy Thanksgiving text message from a number he didn't recognize. Instead of just replying, "Hey, I got a new phone, and I don't have your number saved. Who is this?" he decided to reply with leading questions that he hoped would reveal who sent the text. He finally figured it out, but not without some awkward back-and-forth with the sender.

Then there are those people in our lives who need no introduction. When my wife, Sarah, calls and says, "Hey, it's me," I don't break into cold sweats or strain and struggle to try to place this familiar voice. I know her. I know her voice. We have spent quality time together, and because of that I can know with certainty who is on the other end of the phone.

She doesn't need to reintroduce herself each time she calls. "Hello, Jeremy? This is Sarah, your wife, calling. Perhaps you remember me? We were married September 1, 2007, and we have been sharing every moment of life together since then. Ringing any bells?"

That would be ridiculous. We are past introductions and are well into the deep end of our relationship.

I want this book to help bring us to that place with God, our Father. I want us to know His voice with certainty and confidence each time He speaks. I want God to be able to call you and say, "Hey. It's Me." No introduction necessary.

Do We Recognize Him?

Is it possible that you or I could be in the presence of God Himself—Jesus, the Son of the living God—and not know it was Him? Could He walk in the back door of our church, or come into our office, or jog next to us one morning without us knowing who it was?

Most of us would answer there's no way we wouldn't know—no way. If it were Him, we're just sure we'd know. We'd instantly recognize Him, right? After all, we've seen all His pictures on church walls and bulletins; we've read what He said. We're just sure we'd know it was Him.

Yet I'm not so sure we should be this confident. I'm not convinced we wouldn't just say, "Hey, who's the new guy?" Or just admire His beard.

Something in many of us thinks that a tangible presence of God would impact our lives more than the Holy Spirit's unseen presence. We pray things like, "Jesus, just come into my room tonight and make me know that You are God. Make me know that You are real." Or, "I'm so sick, Jesus. If You would just come into my hospital room and touch me, I know everything would be OK."

We pray and ask Him for His presence, but I think all too often we fail to recognize it when we receive it.

You may be thinking that if you were to see God in person or hear His voice audibly that you would surely know instantly to whom you were talking.

But would you?

What if He weren't wearing His name tag or accompanied by a blinding light or host of angels? What if you didn't get goose bumps? Would you still know beyond any doubt that you were in His presence? Maybe. But maybe not.

We claim to know that Jesus is the Son of God, and we say we believe in Him. But I'm asking you, is it possible that you and I could sit in His presence and not know who it is? Why is it that all too often well-meaning Christians make Him show up in our lives blatantly—with a name tag on that says "Hello. My name is God."—before we ever begin to recognize that it has been Him at work in our lives all along?

This book is dedicated to beginning a study on the character of God Himself because I know there are people asking, "God, where are You? God, why can't I see You in my life?" I don't want Him to have to overwhelm me and leave no doubt He's supernaturally intervening in my life—I want to take the hints before He shows up wearing a name tag I can't possibly miss.

And I want you to join me in this journey of getting to know Him.

We're going to study the character of God so that when we see Him moving in our lives and when nobody else on earth recognizes it's Him, we are going to be quick to say, "This is God. This is the goodness of God. This is the glory of God. This is the love of God. I know it because I know Him."

The Woman at the Well

I want to show you exactly what I am talking about by looking at a passage of Scripture. Let's look at John 4, which contains the story of the woman at the well.

Jesus, tired from a walk to Galilee through Samaria, stops by a well, where He meets a woman who is there to draw water.

John 4:7-10 says,

> A woman of Samaria came to draw water. Jesus said to her, "Give Me a drink." For His disciples had gone away into the city to buy food. Then the woman of Samaria said to Him, "How is it that You, being a Jew, ask a drink from me, a Samaritan woman?" For Jews have no dealings with Samaritans. Jesus answered and said to her, "If you knew the gift of God, and who it is who says to you, 'Give Me a drink,' you would have asked Him, and He would have given you living water."

Three words jump out of the text here—*"if you knew."* In other words, "You don't know."

You don't know who is sitting in front of you. You don't know who you are talking to.

But the living water hint isn't enough, and the conversation goes on. She asks Him how He'll draw water with no bucket, and whether He is greater than their father Jacob, who dug this well. She is turning out to be a little feisty.

Jesus comes back with another clue:

> Whoever drinks of this water will thirst again, but whoever drinks of the water that I shall give him will never thirst. But the water that I shall give him will become in him a fountain of water springing up into everlasting life (John 4:13-14).

That's clue No. 2. He's saying, "Listen, we're not talking about water, water. OK? This is different. The water I'm talking about is everlasting life." He is trying to show Himself to her, to reveal Himself to her through the examples around her.

But she doesn't understand what Jesus is talking about—that He isn't talking about literal water you can draw from a well. Jesus, in fact, isn't really talking about the water she understood at all. He is trying to draw something else out of her entirely.

Why doesn't He just come out and say it? "I'm the Son of God. *Ta-da!*" Why is He talking to her about living-water fountains and everlasting life? Because He is looking for something specific from her. And it's the same thing He is looking for from you and me.

Jesus is endeavoring to solicit from this woman one simple thing—not water, not something to drink, not His own need being met. He is after one thing from her: belief. He wants her to believe in who He is. In a word, what Jesus is after is *faith.* And that hasn't changed—Jesus is still looking for faith and for those who will simply believe He is who He said He is.

Evidently what Jesus tries first to engage her belief does not quite take hold. In the next verse, she asks Him for some of that water so she won't have to go to the well anymore.

She's talking to the Son of God—and she doesn't get it. And I wonder to myself if there are times in our lives when we sit there in the presence of the living God, listening to the subtlety of His voice, and fail to realize to whom we're speaking. However, this is a great example because it shows us Jesus' heart, which of course is a reflection of His Father's. Instead of getting exasperated and moving on to a different well, Jesus keeps after her.

In fact, He tries a different tactic. The whole water analogy didn't seem to quite sink in, so He's going to try a different angle now.

He says, "I'll tell you what, I'll read your mail. We'll get personal. Maybe then you'll understand." Jesus proceeds to tell her all about her life—things He'd have no way of knowing—but again, like many of us, she's completely distracted and misses the point. She does, however, pick up on the outside possibility that this guy who somehow knows the intimate details of her past, having only just met her, *might* be a prophet of some kind. But simply recognizing Jesus as a prophet isn't enough for us, because it isn't enough for Him. He is so much more, and here He's revealing a little more of who He is and where He's coming from, but she misses this, too.

Clearly, Jesus desires to make Himself known to this woman. He wants to introduce her to a life that's new and wonderful, but if she is going to receive anything at all, she is going to have to, at some point, recognize Him for herself.

And that is where faith begins.

But she isn't catching on. In fact, she does something very human—she changes the tone of her conversation. She tries to get "spiritual" with the very Son of God.

"Sir," she says, "I perceive that You are a prophet. Our fathers worshiped on this mountain, and you Jews say that in Jerusalem is the place where one ought to worship" (verse 19). Jesus has just operated in what the Bible calls a word of knowledge (one of the nine gifts of the Spirit found in 1 Corinthians 12), and through Him the Spirit of God revealed insight into this woman's personal life. And how does she respond?

"Sir, I perceive that You are a prophet."

Really? You picked up on that, huh? Then she launches into her beliefs about where people are supposed to worship.

Worship—*she* starts talking to *Him* about worship! "Let's not talk about my scandalous, adulterous past. Let's talk about worship!" You can see what is happening. When the light shines in the darkest corners of her past, her own feelings of guilt and shame take over as she tries to prove something to this apparently religious man before her. You can't really blame her though. She is only being human.

The Cowboy at the Airport

She discovers He's a prophet, so she changes the way she talks. We've all been around people who do this.

When Sarah and I first started dating, we lived in separate states. I went early one morning in March to pick her up at the Dallas/Fort Worth International Airport. She was flying in on a tiny airline, which meant the baggage claim waiting area for this particular flight was completely empty except for me and one other man.

This was Sarah's first trip to see me, so I was very excited. And very early. As I waited there with flowers in my hand, this man walking around the terminal engaged me in conversation.

Well, it wasn't really a conversation. He talked. I listened. He sat there in his straw cowboy hat, blue T-shirt, jeans, and boots and went on and on about, well, him.

"I'm a trucker," he said. "How much money you think I make?" I started to answer with, "I'm really not sure," when he interrupted me with, "A hundred grand a year. That's pretty good, huh?"

This conversation went on for a while, but it wasn't what he said; it was the way he said it. I had never heard that many cuss words all at once. Then he told me all about how he was late getting into Dallas because he had been kicked off the plane in Las Vegas for having had too much to drink and had, evidently, tried to "fire" one of the flight attendants. He apparently didn't realize you actually had to be employed by the airline in a management position. His very colorful story went on for a little while until he said to me, "So, what do you do?"

And I just told him, "I'm a pastor."

"I knew you was a good man," he replied. And I'm thinking, *Wow, thank you. That means so much coming from you.*

"I could tell you was a good man just by talking to ya. You know, I grew up in church, but I hadn't been in a while. I think God wants us to be nice to people, ya know? He doesn't want us looking down on 'em and trying to tell people how to live their lives. Know what I mean?"

"Yeah," I said, "I know what you mean."

It was amazing to me how quickly this man's tone changed when he discovered I was a pastor. A moment before, he was cussing every other word; and now, we are talking about the will of God Almighty for all mankind. No more cussing—suddenly he's this spiritually sensitive individual. The conversation was over in just a few more minutes, but I marveled at how dramatically it had changed when he learned who I was.

God Talk

So Jesus is having a conversation with this Samaritan woman, and she isn't talking to a minister in an airport; she's talking to the Lord of lords and King of kings! She's trying to talk spiritually to the very Son of God. She perceives that He's a spiritual man, so the whole tone of her conversation changes.

The woman at the well and the cowboy/trucker at the airport have something in common. Regardless of their past or present situations, they both have the ability to talk *about* God. Somewhere along the way, they picked up some information about God or religion and began to form opinions. Those opinions became their handy talking points if ever their backs were against the wall in a religious conversation or debate.

I have been on a ministry staff for well over a decade and have been around ministers and ministries my entire life. I have come to realize that most people attending our Christian gatherings get lumped into one of two categories: "Churched" or "Unchurched." They are adjectives that are used, rightly or wrongly, to say how much we think someone does or does not know about God or the Bible, how to act in church, or what they're supposed to wear Sunday morning.

According to these definitions, the woman at the well was not "unchurched." Just listen to what she knows. She knows that Jews and Samaritans are not supposed to talk to each other. That's a denominational line you just don't cross. She also knows enough to give an opinion on where and how someone is supposed to worship God.

•••

HERE'S ANOTHER CLUE: "WOMAN, BELIEVE ME," HE SAYS—EXACTLY WHAT HE'S BEEN AFTER THIS WHOLE TIME.

•••

And Jesus gives a masterful answer to her question by shifting the focus to the spirit and truth of worship, not the mechanics or significance of location. Needless to say, that was the right answer. But does she acknowledge that? No.

Jesus comes right back to her:

Woman, believe Me, the hour is coming when you will
neither on this mountain, nor in Jerusalem, worship
the Father. You worship what you do not know; we
know what we worship, for salvation is of the Jews.
But the hour is coming, and now is, when the true
worshipers will worship the Father in spirit and truth;
for the Father is seeking such to worship Him. God is
Spirit, and those who worship Him must worship in
spirit and truth (John 4:21-24).

Here's another clue: "Woman, believe Me," He says—exactly
what He's been after this whole time. And then look at the language He uses with her. Repeatedly, He talks about Father—
Father, Father, Father. If she had been capable of taking the hint,
putting the fact that He was a prophet together with His refer-
ences to the Father could have tipped her off.

But He drives it home even further, saying that the hour is near
and is in fact *here* when these things will happen.

These words are difficult to translate. So let me instead paint a
picture of what He's saying to her.

Imagine a beautiful young couple who marries right before he is
deployed on a tour of duty in the military. It's an emotional time,
and they're deeply in love. They are together as husband and wife
for such a short time, and then amid tears and farewells, he's off
to the other side of the world.

While he's on station, his young wife notices she's not feeling too
well, notices something is different. And when she finally checks,
finds out she's pregnant! Meanwhile, thousands of miles away, her
husband faces danger—even death—for his country daily.

But then a new order comes through, and in the middle of the
night for some reason, he's woken by his superior officer and told
to pack his bags. He's going home—he's on furlough or being
sent home early for some reason.

But there's such a rush to get to the plane, he doesn't have time to call. He's bundled aboard this military Spartan transport and flies for hours and hours. When he lands, it's the middle of the night, and instead of calling, he gets a cab. He doesn't want to wake her up, and his cell phone is at home anyway, but here he is, drawing closer and closer. First he was in Iraq, then he was in this plane, and now he's in their very city.

But she doesn't know. She doesn't know he's drawing closer and closer, that the time of their reunification is so close.

...

"I AM THE MESSIAH!"
(JOHN 4:26, NLT)

...

She doesn't know his car is pulling onto their street as the sun begins to touch the top of the trees, turning them golden. Maybe she's making an early morning phone call, even talking about her husband, all without knowing that the cab is getting closer.

He pulls up in front of the house, pays the fare, and is striding up the driveway. He reaches the porch, and she still doesn't know. She knows someone is walking up, maybe she's even concerned, but she has no clue it's her husband. He's raising his hand to the doorknob...

He's there—but not quite there yet. He's present, in the now, but they have yet to lay eyes on each other, and she doesn't have a clue.

That is what Jesus is trying to convey to this woman. "The hour is coming, and now is."

But pseudo-religious people are the same now as they were then: They like to argue. Listen to the boldness of her argument in verse 25: "The woman said to Him, 'I know the Messiah is coming' (who is called Christ). 'When He comes, He will tell us all things.'"

She even had enough God-knowledge to talk about the coming Messiah! She knew enough to talk about Him…but not enough to recognize Him as He sat right in front of her.

Maybe it was dawning on her. Maybe here, right at the cusp, she gets it. Because He throws away all pretense, all hints, and says, "I who speak to you am He" (verse 26).

Here's what alarms me—remember where she says she knows the Messiah is coming? She was so close, she even appears to think she'd know Him and was looking for the Messiah. And here He was right in front of her the whole time, unknown. Incognito. At that point in the conversation, she could have been saying, "Well, you have your opinion, Jew, and I have mine."

There she was, talking to the One whom she claims to know about. Uh-oh. *The One she claims to know about.*

I claim to know Him, do you? She is looking for the One, and she didn't even know He was right in front of her.

So she was being cagey right up until the time He plays His trump card, pulling the mask off and revealing Himself.

"Hello," He told her. "My name is God."

If you've wished He would show up in your life, I hope you'll read on to see why I believe there are many Christians like this Samaritan woman, not picking up on Jesus' attempts to solicit belief. I'd like to show you how we can get to know Him so He can get through to us the first time.

Read on and I'll tell you what I mean.

Chapter Three

HEY, IT'S ME!

How can this be? How can someone know so much and yet be so completely clueless? Before we judge this woman too harshly, let's stop and consider ourselves for a moment (a good general practice before judging others).

I know that I, along with many of you reading this, would fall into the same "churched" category as this woman. In fact, in my humble opinion, I think that I am just about as "churched" as someone can get.

I was born into a ministry family; I have grandparents who have been preaching and teaching for over forty years, parents for more than thirty, and I have been at it myself full time since the day I graduated high school. Some of my first complete sentences as a little kid were scriptures. I am very, very churched.

And even though you and I may not share the exact same childhood stories, you may consider yourself churched, too. And if you are at all like me, then you too would like to think that surely you would recognize Jesus Christ, the Son of God, if you ever saw

Him. We would like to think that we would know Him in an instant. After all the services we've sat in, the scriptures we've memorized, and the songs we've sung, surely we should know Him.

•••

WE, AS A BODY, ARE CONFUSED.

•••

But if those things alone were enough to take the blinders off our eyes, we would be living in the most spiritually advanced generation in all of human history. And while in some ways I am sure that we are further along than those that have gone before us, there are other areas in which we seem far behind.

Why do so many struggle to know the plan of God for their lives? Why is there such confusion in His Body over what is of God and what is not? If depth of understanding could be attained by the number of "services sat in," then why do some blame God for something that others say is the devil?

We, as a Body, are confused.

My question is this: Why do we make God show up in our lives with a name tag on before we recognize it's Him? Why does He have to show up and say, "The one you're talking to and the one you're talking about—it's Me"? Maybe if we find out what was blinding the woman at the well, we will discover what has kept so many in confusion and hindered our ability to recognize Him, His voice, His purpose, and His will for our lives.

Is it possible to have a conversation with Jesus the Christ, the Son of the living God, and have no idea who you're talking to—even when you're looking for Him? Yes.

And all along the way, Jesus is trying to solicit belief from this woman. Do you think He's doing anything different with you and me today? He's still looking for one thing from you and me. Belief—the recognition of who He is, where He comes from, whom He belongs to, and what He's done for you and me.

And I'm not just talking about the belief one can have when you're right there in the middle of God's obvious presence.

•••

I'M LOOKING FOR THAT, "HEY! IT'S ME!" RELATIONSHIP WITH GOD.

•••

Yet how often does God *not* show up in power and majesty, obviously putting Himself on display? And of those times, how often do we fail to recognize Him when He has indeed shown up?

How often must He say, "Hello. My name is God," before we bother to notice Him?

You see, I'm looking for that, "Hey! It's Me!" relationship with God. I want the kind of relationship with Him where if He were to call on the phone and just say, "Hey! It's Me!" I'd instantly know who it was.

The all-too-common alternative is that when He calls, we don't know who is on the other end of the line.

But we also all have people with whom we are on that level— that without preamble or introduction we can call, caller ID or not, who will recognize our voices instantly. Parents, siblings, friends—they *know* you.

With these people, you don't reintroduce yourself so they know who is calling. You don't call your mother and say, "Hello, Mother. This is your daughter, Sally—the one born to you thirty-seven years ago. Perhaps you remember me from that incident in the first grade?"

We all have people in our lives whom we can call and say, "Hey! It's me!" and without a word more, they know who we are by the sounds of our voices, and if we were to call them, they could do the same. Not only do we know them, but they know us. We have a relationship together with shared history. We've been through common experiences.

I want to be there with God. I want Him to be able to show up in my life in the most subtle of ways—the tone of His voice, the way He speaks, whatever—and tip me off it's Him, without introduction and without Him wearing a bright orange name tag that says, "Hello. My name is God."

So why is it that so often God calls on our lives, but we fail to recognize His voice? Why don't we get His hints?

Point-blank, I think we don't get them because we're just not that familiar with Him.

Ouch.

•••

BY EXPLORING HIS CHARACTER TOGETHER, WE WILL BEGIN TO RECOGNIZE HIM BETTER.

•••

Why?

I asked the Lord about this. I said, "What is it that we're missing? Why don't we know it's You when You call?" Of course, that's what this whole book is about, but let's look at the results—why we are failing to see and recognize Him when He calls on us.

In a nutshell, it's all about His character. The very traits each section of this book deals with were a revelation about His goodness and character that came from asking the question, "Why?" of Him over and over.

He began to share with me about character qualities we're not quick to recognize in Him, about ways of revealing Himself that we are often slow to see because we don't really know Him as well as we think we do. I want to know when God shows up subtly in my life, calling without introducing Himself, and I believe that by exploring His character together, we will begin to recognize Him better.

Wouldn't you like to be able to see God move in your life and know it's Him? To know His voice, recognize the way He moves? Wouldn't you like to understand His goodness, His love, and His character more? Wouldn't you like His voice to stand out above all the others of this world, clearer than any other, so you can obey, agree, and be a good and faithful servant?

I know I would.

Let's do it together.

SECTION II

GOODNESS
&
MERCY

Chapter Four

A CONVERSATION WITH LOVE HIMSELF

So you're still reading—that's good.

Want to recognize God more quickly? I know you want to know our God of love, and somewhat amazingly, He wants you to know Him, as well, just as Jesus wanted the woman at the well to know Him as Messiah.

We don't know a lot about the Samaritan woman Jesus met at the well other than what the Spirit of God revealed to Jesus regarding her past and present circumstances. He showed Jesus that she had been married five times and was now with a man who was not her husband. It is clear to me that her inability to recognize Jesus was directly related to her love life.

I want to explain this by bringing her situation into our modern world. I realize that can't always be done with Scripture and that we can often find deeper truths by endeavoring to understand the environment in which the words were originally spoken. However, it seems to me that no one—no matter the day and age she lives in—can endure five marriages and five divorces without coming out on the other end with, at least, a slightly skewed concept of love.

•••

NO ONE CAN ENDURE FIVE MARRIAGES WITHOUT COMING OUT WITH A SLIGHTLY SKEWED CONCEPT OF LOVE.

•••

Imagine this were a woman living today. What if she, like so many others, had begun dreaming as a young girl about the perfect man who would one day come and sweep her away to be husband and wife forever and ever? And then she meets him. He swears his love to her and says all the right things. He makes promises of a life together, and she says to herself, "This must be it. This must be love." Then comes the wedding day, and it's everything she dreamed it would be.

But like so many love stories today, somewhere along the line this one takes a wrong turn. He is not the man she thought he was—and much less the man he promised to be. What was supposed to be love is revealed to be lies or abuse or cheating or strife. And because the marriage covenant seems to be worth so little, she is tossed aside and is now dealing with the heartache and pain of a bitter divorce.

Sometime later, she finds herself telling her sad story to another man because he seems like someone she could trust. He looks deep into her eyes and says, "He was a fool to treat you that way, and I will never do those things to you. I love you."

Despite her apprehension, she decides to try loving again and finds herself once more at the altar of marriage. But what began as hope for restoration soon turns into an all-too-familiar battle for her soul. Again, she is being lied to and lied about and cheated on.

"Is this possible?" she asks herself. "Can this be happening to me again?"

But it is happening to her again, and it happens to her again, and again, and again. Each time around, another man promises to love and then bitterly disappoints her. Until finally, when the man she is with now begins making some of those same promises to love her forever, she stops him and says, "Save it. Let's not make this more than what it is. There is no such thing as love. At least not for me."

So what does this have to do with her inability to recognize Jesus as the Messiah? First John 4:8 says, "But anyone who does not love does not know God, for God is love" (NLT).

Do you remember the three key words Jesus said to this woman at the onset of their conversation? He said, "If you knew…" In other words, "You don't know."

Her concept of love had been so violently distorted that there she sat having a conversation with Love Himself, yet had no idea to whom she was talking.

I know I have taken liberty by looking into this woman's story in a way that is not printed in Scripture. Though this account occurred thousands of years ago, I just can't help but recognize there are people living the same story today. There are those who have hurt or been hurt in unimaginable ways, and they feel that their experience excludes them from the opportunity to love or be loved ever again.

While her story may not be your story, the truth remains the same. If you don't know how to recognize and receive the unconditional, undying, unwavering love of God, then you will never be able to know with certainty when He is speaking to you or leading you by His Holy Spirit.

We are at the beginning of our study of the character of God and the reputation behind His Name, and there is a reason we have to talk about love first. It is because this is who He *is*. At the beginning of this book, I told you we would be filling in the

blank: God is _____. We must begin by filling the blank
with *Love*. We are loved. You are loved.

"Yeah, yeah," I can hear you saying.

Don't say that. Don't act like this is all something you have
heard before. Even if you have heard it before, you need to hear it
again. You need to hear that you are precious and priceless in the
eyes of our Father. You also need to know that there is a difference between having heard you are loved and *believing* you are
loved. That same chapter of 1 John says that we have known *and*
believed the love that God has for us.

Yeah, I know you have heard all this; but do you *believe* all this?
Do you believe that He is a God of love, who is only capable of—
and solely motivated by—His great love for you? It's true.

Let me ask you a question. Are you one of those people who
often tells God, yourself, and others how "unworthy" you are? If
you are, stop it! You are not the one who gets to determine what
you are worth. Can you see the connection in those two words?
When you say, "God, I'm so un*worthy*," you are saying, "God,
I'm so not *worth* it."

Hidden Treasure

Jesus used a parable in the book of Matthew to give us an
understanding of what the kingdom of heaven is all about. He said
there was a man who found a great treasure hidden in the ground.
When he found it, he was so excited that he reburied it in the field
and went to sell everything he had so he could buy that field.

Can you imagine selling everything you have to buy a *field*? You
could if you knew there was treasure buried there!

Imagine that guy coming home from work and running into his
house to tell his wife that she needs to gather up everything they
own because they are selling all of it.

"We are getting rid of everything!" he exclaims. "Furniture, dishes, clothes, cars, your mother. It all has to go!"

"Wait just a minute here!" she says. "What has gotten into you? Why are you selling all of our stuff?"

•••

THE PRICE PAID DETERMINES
THE VALUE.

•••

"Sweetheart," he replies, bursting with excitement, "I'm buy-ing…a *field!*"

Now if she doesn't know about the treasure, then she is prob-ably wondering what has gotten into her husband and thinking that her family was right all along. He *is* crazy!

If you or anyone else were walking past that field, you may look at it and see only a patch of grass, dirt, and rocks. But because this man sees the treasure hidden beneath the surface, he is will-ing to pay everything he owns. Once the man owns the field, that worthless patch of grass now becomes worth everything to him. Why? Because that is what he paid for it. The price paid deter-mines the value.

You're Worth the Price

First Corinthians 6:20 says that *you* were bought with a price. Someone gave all He had so that He could have you. You may look at yourself and see worthlessness, but the truth is you are worth the price that was paid for you.

So who would do that? Who is crazy enough to give all they have just to have you? God is. He is so crazy in love with you that He said you were worth the price He paid.

And what was that price? It was the life, death, and resurrection of His Son, Jesus. You were worth every stripe on His back. You were worth the agonizing pain of the crucifixion.

Every drop of His spilled blood cried out, "I love you! I have loved you from before the foundations of the earth!"

Maybe you have been looking in the mirror every day at what you think is worthless, but you need to fix your eyes on the treasure hidden beneath the surface. That is the real you. And the real you is loved with a love this world doesn't know. The love most are familiar with is a love that says, "If you do for me, I'll do for you. If you don't for me, I won't for you." But the God kind of love says, "What I did for you, I did before you ever knew Me."

Again, 1 John 4:10 says, "This is real love—not that we loved God, but that he loved us and sent his Son as a sacrifice to take away our sins" (NLT).

I heard my mother say once, "Never let what anyone else has done *to* you be bigger than what Jesus has done *for* you." Maybe you are more like this woman at the well than you first realized. Perhaps someone has said or done something to you that has severely damaged your ability to show or feel love. The best and most sure way out of that hurt is to begin to believe that God Himself loves you. Get past what you think you know and begin to believe in this love on a whole new level. Stop thinking about what you have or haven't done and think only about what He has done. Solely motivated by love, He paid the highest price for you—and you are worth it.

Know Love

If you want to know God, then this is where you must begin. Without an understanding of His great love, you will be limited to only knowing *about* God and never really knowing Him.

"Oh, Jeremy," you may be saying, "we could never *understand* God's love for us."

That's not what the Bible says. Paul prays for us in Ephesians 3:18-19 that we would be able to comprehend with all the saints what is the breadth and length and depth and height of God's love for us and to know the love of Christ, which passes all knowledge. These words talk about comprehending and knowing the love of Christ. If you comprehend the breadth, length, depth, and height of anything, then that means you have a working knowledge of what it is, where it came from, what it does, and how to use it.

•••

INTIMATE KNOWLEDGE OF
GOD BEGINS WITH INTIMATE
KNOWLEDGE OF HIS LOVE.

•••

Is it possible to have that kind of comprehension of something so vast and expansive as the love of God? Yes! But notice he said it is a love that passes knowledge. *The Amplified Bible* makes this clearer by stating it this way in verse 19:

> [That you may really come] to know [practically, through experience for yourselves] the love of Christ, which far surpasses mere knowledge [without experience]; that you may be filled [through all your being] unto all the fullness of God [may have the richest measure of the divine Presence, and become a body wholly filled and flooded with God Himself]!

That's it! We come to know Him through the experiential knowledge of His love. Will we ever exhaust all there is to know about God and His great love? Probably not. But that doesn't mean we shouldn't know more today than we did yesterday; and tomorrow we should experience more than we ever have before. Your last day on planet earth should be the greatest experience in the presence of God you've ever had up until that moment when you see Him face to face.

Intimate knowledge of God begins with intimate knowledge of His love.

Everything Springs From His Love

God's love for us will be the foundation for the rest of our study through this book. We will view everything through the filter of this amazing love. How are we going to recognize His voice if we don't first recognize that everything He will ever say to us comes from this place of love?

Right now He is calling you saying, "Hey. It's Me, and I want you to know how much I love you."

What is your response? Is it, "Who is this? Your voice is familiar… Do I know you?"

If you don't know love, then you don't know God. But if you have what the Bible calls experiential knowledge of His great love, then you will reply with confidence and no hesitation, "Thank You, Lord, for loving me. I believe Your love and I receive Your love."

This begins a beautiful conversation in which God can begin to reveal to you the greatness of the treasure hidden just below your surface. This concept may be easy to accept for some, but it may prove more difficult to others. Everyone has a different story and has lived through different experiences. The Scripture tells us that Jesus came to preach peace to them who were near *and* to them that were far off. It does not matter where you think you are (or are not) in your walk with God. His love has been extended to all and knows no boundaries.

If you're still skeptical, that's OK. We've got the rest of the book and beyond to get it figured out. I am, however, going to offer one final proof for the love of God before we go on to the next chapter. What I am about to tell you is the result of intense research and will require your complete attention. Open now your heart, your mind, and your eyes in an effort to fully understand the depths of what I am about to say. This is going to be deep. Ready? Here goes.

How do I *know* God loves me? Because the Bible tells me so.

Call me crazy, but I am one of those people who reads *and* believes the Bible. I believe it is God's Word and thus a revelation of who He is. And who is that?

God is **LOVE.**

Let's take a look together at exactly how good God is...

Chapter Five

Good God

There is a God.

Although that statement may seem harmless, it is under greater attack than ever before. People who believe in the existence of God as the Creator and the Source of life are being persecuted and mocked in the classroom, in the boardroom, and in the newsroom.

In spite of the mockery, I believe that statement. I am so convinced there is a God that no one could talk me out of it. And try as they may, they can't shame me out of that belief, either. I believe with all my heart and from the depths of me that He is real. I sincerely hope that you and I are agreed on this point.

We will be discussing a more comprehensive insight into the character of God, and acknowledging the existence of God could seem somewhat "beginner." But in order to understand Him on a deeper level, we're going to start by going back to what we already know to be true about Him.

I believe you will find that simply acknowledging His existence and His presence is more powerful and profound than you might at first think. Proverbs 3 tells us that if we will acknowledge Him in all our ways, He will direct our paths. We can and should be living lives that God directs, and that begins by simply acknowledging Him in everything.

•••

MOST PEOPLE ASSOCIATE FAITH
WITH THE UNKNOWN, BUT IT REALLY
ONLY PERTAINS TO THE UNSEEN.

•••

It is as simple as saying, "Good morning, Lord. This is the day that You have made. I will live it knowing that You are God who loves me." You have just acknowledged God. Now do that several more times today, tomorrow, and the next day.

If you're looking for life direction, then I would begin right here—at the beginning. There is more power in simply acknowledging the reality of God than you might think. If it were any less important, I guarantee we wouldn't be witnessing the all-out war against our conviction that there really is a God.

We are beginning with acknowledging that God exists, because that's where He begins. The Bible actually tells us that if you are going to come to God, you must first believe that He exists (Hebrews 11:6). That is faith in its most basic form—believe He exists.

It will help you to stop thinking of faith simply as a set of religious ideals. Faith is substance and evidence. In Hebrews 11, the writer defines faith for us in verse 1: "Faith is the substance of things hoped for, the evidence of things not seen."

Most people associate faith with the unknown, but it really only pertains to the unseen. So instead of thinking of God as "unknown," just think of Him as "unseen." According to Hebrews 11:1, there is evidence for things we can't see naturally.

You may have heard this before, but I like the story of the kindergarten teacher and her student. A kindergarten teacher was observing her classroom of children while they were drawing. She occasionally walked around to see each child's work. As she got to one little girl who was working diligently, she asked what the drawing was.

The girl replied, "I'm drawing God."

The teacher paused and said, "But no one knows what God looks like."

Without missing a beat, or looking up from her drawing, the girl replied, "They will in a minute."

We can't see God, but there is plenty of evidence for His existence. In fact, Romans tells us,

> They know the truth about God because he has made it obvious to them. For ever since the world was created, people have seen the earth and sky. Through everything God made, they can clearly see his invisible qualities—his eternal power and divine nature. So they have no excuse for not knowing God (Romans 1:19-20, NLT).

Go look out the nearest window. You probably won't see God Himself standing there waving, but if you look, you will find evidence that He is real. This scripture says that creation is revealing God to us. He spoke our world into existence, and whether or not you believe that fact, it's a big deal.

The rest of Romans 1 goes on to tell us what kind of life stems from choosing to believe that God doesn't exist or is not the Creator. It tells us that they knew God but would not worship Him or give Him thanks, and then they began to make up stupid and foolish ideas (the Bible's words, not mine) of what God was like. The end result was that their minds became dark and *confused.*

I believe that one of Satan's highest priorities is keeping

Christians confused. And as I mentioned earlier, I believe that we as a Body have been confused far too long. One part of the Body says that the hurricane was God judging people, and another part says that God is not the destroyer but that Satan is the one killing people. If we can't tell the difference between God and the devil, then we are confused.

I am on a campaign to get rid of confusion. Won't you join me? How do we do it? We become so familiar with the true nature of God through the study of His Word and time in His presence that we can never again be talked into something that is not the truth.

Second Corinthians 10:3 says that even though we walk after the flesh, we don't war after the flesh—we are in the world, but we don't make war with the world's weapons. That means that even though we as Christians are not in a fight with other people, we are indeed in a fight.

Paul then goes on to tell us that God has given us weapons to fight with. And what do those weapons do? They pull down strongholds, and cast down arguments of human reasoning and false arguments and every high and proud thing that exalts itself against the knowledge of God and keeps people from knowing God.

Did you catch that? The fight is against our knowledge of God. Evidently, God is not surprised by Satan's attack against His existence disguised as human reasoning. He knew it was coming. That's why He gave us the weapons to fight it.

So now you see why I say there is an all-out war against our conviction that God is real. And you also see why I boldly and passionately proclaim my deep-seated belief that there is a God. Knowing Him intimately begins there.

God Is and God Gives

But where do we go from here? Polls tell us most Americans at least still believe there is a God, but we have trouble agreeing beyond that. Millions and millions believe in the existence of God, so why is there still so much confusion?

While believing God is real is vitally important, it is not the end of the journey.

One of my all-time favorite scriptures is found in Hebrews 11:6. Listen to what it says: "And it is impossible to please God without faith. Anyone who wants to come to him must…" (NLT). Now pay careful attention here. The writer is about to tell us what it takes to come to God. He says anyone who wants to come to God *must.* *Must* what? "Anyone who wants to come to him must believe…."

•••

YOU DON'T HAVE TO GET
YOURSELF ALL CLEANED AND
FIXED UP BEFORE YOU GO TO HIM.

•••

You must *believe.* I love it! This is what God is looking for. This is faith, and faith is what pleases Him. It's not a long list of good works that He demands before you are worthy to come to Him. You don't have to get yourself all cleaned and fixed up before you go to Him.

He is looking for those who will believe. Believe what? According to Hebrews 11:6 (NLT), faith is believing and believing two things: "Anyone who wants to come to him must believe that God exists…." There it is again.

So you must believe that He is—that He exists. In other words, you believe that there *is* a God. You believe that He is real. You believe that when you fall to your knees and pray, that you are not just talking to the air. You believe you're talking to a God who loves you, who gave Himself for you. You're talking to the Creator of heaven and earth. You're talking to the One who, through His own words, released creative power and made everything. You're talking to the One who put life and breath in your lungs today.

Think about it as you take your next breath—inhale, then let it out. He is the One who gave you that breath and every one that came before it and after it. The One who gave you that, that's the One you're talking to. You must believe that He is.

So first of all, faith is believing. It's saying, "I believe there is a God. I believe there was a God and there always will be a God. I believe that Jesus Christ is the same yesterday, today, and forever." This is all believing that *He is*.

Believing in the existence of God is fundamental to a deeper revelation of His character and true nature.

So we have established our belief that there is a God—that's one. What is next? "Anyone who wants to come to him must believe that God exists and that he rewards those who sincerely seek him" (NLT). The second thing we read in Hebrews is that when you come to God, you must believe that He is a rewarder of those who diligently seek Him. This is not optional.

We must believe He is, and we must believe He is a rewarder. I like to say it like this: "God is. And God gives."

•••

FAITH ACCEPTS HIS GOODNESS TOWARD US
IN THE FORM OF HIS SON, JESUS.

•••

Maybe you are one of the millions who believe there is a God. That is a great start. But are you one of the few who will take your relationship with Him to deeper levels by believing He is a good and giving God?

Hebrews 11:6 could have said anything. It could have said that if we want to come to God, we must believe that He is, and that He'll strike us down when we mess up. Or, it could have said that we must believe that He is, and we'd better get our act together and do some major cleanup if we expect Him to have anything to do with us.

But it didn't say that. He said that we must believe that He is, and that He is good. So many people have put themselves under the undue burden of trying to please God through works and deeds when all along He was simply looking for faith.

"But I thought faith without works was dead," you may be saying. It is. But I also believe that works, without faith, is *death*. You will kill yourself trying to be "good enough" for God.

Faith accepts His goodness toward us in the form of His Son, Jesus.

Now live life based on what you believe. If you believe God is good, then why would you be fearful when it comes to being obedient to Him? If He is good, then His plan for you is good. If He is good, then His will for you is good.

God spoke through the prophet Jeremiah and said, "I know the plans I have for you. They are good and not evil. They are plans for a bright and brilliant future."

The goodness of God is not something we can debate. It is a truth that is to be accepted no matter what argument or high thing would exalt itself against it. God is good. He is a good God. And as convinced as you and I are that He exists, we should be that convinced that He is a rewarder of them who seek Him.

He is looking for belief in His existence and goodness from those who would come to Him. Why? Because this insight into His character is a key to understanding Him.

The "Good" Guy

An illustration from Jesus' life perfectly communicates what I am endeavoring to show you:

> Now as He was going out on the road, one came running, knelt before Him, and asked Him, "Good Teacher, what shall I do that I may inherit eternal life?" So Jesus said to him, "Why do you call me good? No one is good but One, that is God" (Mark 10:17-18).

For a long time I was puzzled by Jesus' response to this man. It was strange to me that Jesus would ask why he called Him good. Of course Jesus never took glory to Himself for anything but always drew men's attention back to His Father, so that part made sense. But isn't Jesus "good" too? As I studied this I found this whole account centers around that word *good.* Jesus went on to say to him,

> "You know the commandments: 'Do not commit adultery,' 'Do not murder,' 'Do not steal,' 'Do not bear false witness,' 'Do not defraud,' 'Honor your father and your mother.'" And he answered and said to Him, "Teacher, all these things I have kept from my youth." Then Jesus, looking at him, loved him, and said to him, "One thing you lack: Go your way, sell whatever you have and give to the poor, and you will have treasure in heaven; and come, take up the cross, and follow Me" (verses 19-21).

The Bible tells us this man was sad when he heard this and went away sad because he was very wealthy.

So what happened here? Clearly this man has a sincere desire for eternal life, and has come to the right place to get his question answered.

But notice how he addressed Jesus: "Good teacher." Is he coming to Jesus because he believes Jesus is the Messiah, the Son of the living God? No. He is coming to Jesus because he believes Jesus is a "good teacher."

It's not enough to just believe that Jesus was simply a "good teacher." He wasn't just a wise man, a good guy, a prophet, or one of the best people to walk the planet.

He is THE Way, THE Truth, THE Life, and He's THE ONLY way to the Father. Put bluntly, believing anything less than that is not Christianity and will not result in eternal life.

We could also say from Matthew's account that this man further misunderstood the word "good" when he asks Jesus what "good" thing can he *do* to inherit eternal life.

The message of Jesus Christ is not salvation through *doing good.* It is salvation through *believing* the good thing that *God has done for us* through sending Jesus. That is the standard of "good," and everything else pales in comparison to that good gift.

You can see from this story that just keeping commandments is not enough for salvation—it's not enough to satisfy a sincere heart that is longing for truth and eternal life. This man told Jesus he had kept all the commandments from the time he was young.

He is saying, "There has to be more. I've *done* everything I can *do,* and still I know something is missing!" Jesus then told him he was still lacking one thing. He told him to sell what he had, give to the poor, then come follow Him.

But because this man had a misconception of what was truly "good," he went away sorrowful. To him, the goodness of Jesus' teaching wasn't as good as the goodness of having his money. He, like the woman at the well, was in search of love, yet he was unable to recognize Love Himself; he was in search of good but was unable to recognize the goodness of God extended to him in the invitation to follow Jesus.

As good as it can be to have some money, it doesn't begin to compare to the goodness of knowing and following God. Had this man simply placed his faith in the goodness of God, he would have soon found that God is a rewarder of those who follow Him.

Jesus went on to say to His disciples, after this rich man walked away, that no one has left anything for His sake and the gospel's who will not receive a hundredfold now in this lifetime. What a promise! This man could have received a hundredfold return had he been willing to give what Jesus asked.

If you fail to recognize that God gives and rewards because He is good—not because you worked for it—then you, like this rich man, will be reluctant to obey the leadership of the Holy Spirit when it comes time to give, or to speak, or to move out in His plan for you.

God's leadership shouldn't scare you; it should excite you. It should thrill you to hear from Him knowing that He always leads us forward and never backward. Never hold on to anything because you think that this is as good as it gets. In God, it only gets better.

•••

JESUS DIDN'T "SPELL IT OUT."
HE SIMPLY SAID, "FOLLOW ME."

•••

God's Good

You probably think it would be more convenient if God would just spell things out for you. "Tell me why, God, You are asking me to give this! When will I get a hundredfold return? Is it going to come quickly? Can You give me a date I can expect the check in the mail?"

But notice Jesus didn't "spell it out" to this man either. He simply said, "Follow Me." Why?

Because following Him based solely on His Word is called faith, and faith is what He is looking for. Again, faith doesn't deal with the unknown, only the unseen. Just because you can't see the hundredfold return yet doesn't mean there isn't evidence for it. You can know that it is true because He said it was true, and our good God doesn't lie.

As I was studying these things, I asked the Lord what this man lacked. I believe the Lord answered me that this man lacked the revelation of the goodness of God. He knew plenty about good works but nothing about the true nature of God.

What do you suppose would have happened had this man been obedient to the call of God? As he followed Jesus, he would have built the rest of his life upon firsthand experiential knowledge of the goodness of God. But he missed it because of an improper view of what is truly good.

I was speaking to a congregation once about some of these same things. I wanted them to begin to see how our concept of what is good needed to come to a higher level. I asked all the men in the crowd, who among them could raise their hand and say that they drove a "good truck"?

As this congregation was in Texas, there were a lot of hands that went up. I then asked how many of those same men that would say they have a "good truck" would also say that they have a "good wife."

"You do realize there is a difference, don't you?" I asked.

Though we use the same word to describe both a truck and a wife, there is a vast difference in the meaning of the word. I happen to have both a "good truck" and a "good wife." But they are not in the same category of good.

I'm thankful to have a truck that runs well, but it does not begin to compare to how eternally thankful and grateful I am for my wonderful wife, Sarah. Other than Jesus, she is the greatest expression of the goodness of God toward me I've ever known, and I would be a fool to put a stupid truck, or car, or house, or anything else up next to her. They don't even compare.

And in the same way, nothing on this earth can compare to the overwhelming goodness of God. The good stuff you own doesn't compare to the good He wants to bless you with.

How do we receive the things He wants to bless us with? By faith. By believing that He has already blessed us and given us richly all things to enjoy.

The good works you've done don't compare to the good works God has accomplished through Jesus. That is why salvation is for us who believe by faith that everything Jesus did, He did for us. His works on the Cross and in death, hell, and the grave were all done so we wouldn't have to.

And now His resurrection life can live big in us when we simply receive by faith all that has been accomplished through Him. God is so good!

Hebrews 11:6 is so crystal clear about what it takes to come to God. Again, He does not require a laundry list of good works and self-sacrifice. He requires faith. That has been His requirement all along. He was, is, and always will be looking for people who will take Him at His Word—people who will believe it simply because He said it.

That is what it means to believe. Believe what?

God is GOOD.

•••

GOD WASN'T IN THE WIND,
EARTHQUAKE, OR FIRE.
HE WAS IN A STILL, SMALL VOICE.

•••

In the Whisper

So can we be in the very presence of God and not know it's Him? I'd say we've established that yes, we can.

I'd like to suggest that one of the main reasons we sometimes fail to recognize Him until He pulls out all the stops is that we don't really know what He's like. We don't know what His voice sounds like.

I'd like to take a few scriptures and look at them. Let's start with 1 Kings 19:11-12:

> Then He said, "Go out, and stand on the mountain before the Lord." And behold, the Lord passed by, and a great and strong wind tore into the mountains and broke the rocks in pieces before the Lord, but the Lord was not in the wind; and after the wind an earthquake, but the Lord was not in the earthquake; and after the earthquake a fire, but the Lord was not in the fire; and after the fire a still small voice.

God wasn't in the wind, the earthquake, or the fire. He was in a still, small voice.

Do we know that voice? Can we get quiet enough? Can we become familiar enough with God to recognize Him when all He does is whisper?

Take a moment and read Psalm 46—the whole thing. It's bookended by verses we've heard many times before: "God is our refuge and strength, a very present help in trouble" and "Be still, and know that I am God" (verses 1, 10). But in between, the mountains are crumbling into the sea; the oceans are roaring and foaming; the nations are in chaos.

What we read in the middle isn't too different than what Isaiah saw—the earth moving, the mountains crashing and quaking.

And in it all, God tells us, "Be still, and know that I am God."

Sometimes it seems we are out there looking for anything and everything that might be God, and all the time He's telling us to simply be still and stop running around.

God isn't in the hurricanes, the earthquakes, the fires; He's not in the tsunamis, the wildfires, the mudslides. And yet what do we call these things? "Acts of God." It makes you wonder if we really know Him very well at all if our very term for these things reveals how *little* we know about Him.

I live in North Central Texas, and every spring—and sometimes, fall—we get tornadoes ripping through Texas, Oklahoma, and other states in the so-called "Tornado Alley." Inevitably, you see somebody from some little town in the middle of nowhere on national television talking about what the tornado sounded like.

•••

GOD TELLS US, "BE STILL,
AND KNOW THAT I AM GOD."

•••

But the thing that really amazes me about all of that is they will stand there and say, "I don't know why God did this to us." And the newspeople will do the same thing—they'll call it an act of God and try to find some forlorn people standing in front of their demolished church. People who won't spend another hour endeavoring to know God's will and His plans will question His purpose for letting—or worse, *causing*—this tornado to destroy their town. Or someone will try to explain all of it away as though it was the will of God.

If I were God, I wouldn't appreciate that very much. I know I don't like it when someone who really doesn't know me, with whom I don't share a lot of common experience, tries to speak for me as though they knew me and understood my intentions. It bothers me.

We are missing something very basic about the character of God. Something has deluded our concept of what God is like, has infected it with an idea that God is flashy, and vengeful, and destructive when angry.

Yet Elijah discovered that God wasn't in the wind. He wasn't in the earthquake. He wasn't in the fire.

The Lord was in the still, small voice.

But the Lord knows that those of us who don't listen—who are so expecting the spectacle of wind and shaking and fire—won't recognize Him unless He eventually shows up with His name tag on. Instead of speaking quietly into our spirits, He finally has to show up and say, "I've been trying to get you to believe all along. I've been showing you this. I've been telling you that, and all along that was Me…and you weren't listening! You didn't know it was Me!"

Does God Speak?

I firmly believe we have no idea how merciful God really is to us. We don't have any idea how many times He saved us and we didn't even know there was danger, or how many times He spared us from something eminent and destructive, and we never knew the peril we were in.

I started to pick up on this one day when Sarah and I were getting ready to head from our home to church. When she and I were youth pastors, we spent our Wednesdays at home preparing for that evening's service. Typically, she would leave for church a couple of hours before me because she was leading our worship team and needed to be there for pre-service rehearsal.

This particular day, I was beginning a series called "Hearing the Voice of God" and had been home all day trying to prepare. I say "trying" because it seemed like I was getting nowhere in my message preparation. I couldn't find a good place to start.

Though I believe with all my heart that God does indeed speak
to me and anyone who will listen, I had never before taught
others "how" to hear. It wasn't like I couldn't think of anything
to say, I just couldn't think of the right thing to say.

...

"DOES GOD SPEAK?"
THE ANSWER IS, UNDENIABLY, "YES, HE DOES."

...

"Where do I begin?" I asked myself. "I know God speaks
through His Word, through the leadership of His Spirit, through
His ministry gifts. But where do I start?" Nothing seemed right.
Every time I would make a note, I sensed the Lord telling me to
back up. He was instructing me to get as basic as I possibly could.
But for some reason I was stuck.

Meanwhile, Sarah was getting in the car to leave, and I was
standing in the garage saying goodbye when I heard this small
voice inside say, "Don't let Sarah drive tonight." This was not
a booming, amplified, surround-sound kind of voice. This was
something very small and subtle.

Small enough that I could rationalize it away and say to myself,
"I don't have time to take her. I have to stay here and try to figure
out what I am going to say about hearing the voice of God." Brilliant, huh?

Sarah drove away and I retreated back to my study. Then, ten
minutes later, my phone rang. It was Sarah. She had been in an
accident. I jumped in my truck and drove to meet her between
our house and the church. Praise God, she was all right! It was
truly remarkable.

As she was driving, a truck pulled out in front of her. This truck
was towing another truck with an eight-foot yellow strap. For some
reason, the driver thought that he could get his truck—and the one
behind him—in front of her before she passed. He was wrong.

But instead of hitting either of the trucks, Sarah drove straight *between* them, with that yellow strap causing minimal front-end damage to her car. God is merciful to Jeremy—and to Sarah, who was impacted by my unwillingness to hear God's voice!

I found my message for that evening. I began by asking our teenagers, "Does God speak?" And the answer is, undeniably, "Yes, He does."

It left me asking the Holy Ghost, "Open my eyes. Show me. Show me what You've done for me. Show me. I want to see it so I can praise You for it, and so I can become aware and get to know You."

I want you to be thinking about this story. I am going to bring it up again in the "Help Wanted" section.

His Mercy Endures Forever

I have often wondered why God's mercy is such a foreign concept to us—why even Christians should be so quick to ascribe God the personality of a vengeful, smiting deity.

So much evidence in the Bible points to the contrary; just take a look at Psalm 136:1-3:

> Oh, give thanks to the Lord, for He is good!
> *For His mercy endures forever.*
> Oh, give thanks to the God of gods!
> *For His mercy endures forever.*
> Oh, give thanks to the Lord of lords!
> *For His mercy endures forever.*

The whole psalm goes on like this! In fact, I think it's safe to say that we can identify the central theme to this psalm pretty easily. You don't need a theology degree or years of study to figure it out.

God's *mercy* endures forever.

I love the way the psalmist lays it out, how he begins: *"Give thanks to the Lord, for He is good!"* He goes through from the very moment of Creation, telling us that from the time God put the sun in the sky, His mercy was already enduring forever. Mercy was there on day one! The entire psalm is a thorough case study in God's mercy throughout the life of His people.

We have something to be thankful for every day, every moment—God is good, and His mercy endures forever!

•••

DESPITE WHAT WE HAVE THROWN AT IT,
DESPITE THE WARS THAT RAGE IN OUR LIVES,
DESPITE OUR FAILINGS, HIS MERCY ENDURES.
IT IS NOT ABOUT TO RUN OUT.

•••

I'm going to ask you to indulge me for a moment: Go get your Bible so you can read this psalm in its entirety. Seriously—grab it. But be careful—it's easy to begin to glaze over the refrain, that His mercy endures forever—so I challenge you to read it with intention and let it sink in. This is the way the psalmist is urging his people to remember the Lord—for His enduring mercy.

Before you begin, let me give you a trick I use whenever I find a phrase like this or a statement like this. I pick it apart one word at a time, putting emphasis on a different word each time I read it.

"His mercy endures forever." Whose? *God's* mercy endures forever. This isn't another human telling you that you are forgiven. This is God saying it! This is mercy that is coming from the highest authority. Is there anyone who can overturn His ruling? No! His Word is final authority, and He will not go back on it.

Now notice what is enduring. Is it His anger or wrath? No! His *compassion* and *forgiveness* endures forever! Psalm 103 says that God is merciful and gracious and *slow* to anger and abounding in mercy. The psalmist also tells us that His anger endures but for a moment.

Does that sound like the God of traditional religious thinking? Does that sound like God is watching you just waiting for you to mess it all up so He can "smite" you a good one? If that has been your concept of God, then I suggest you start thinking about what the Bible actually says instead. The Bible says it's His mercy that endures over you. Not His anger—mercy.

What does His mercy do? It endures—it goes on, it perseveres, it suffers through. We marvel at old buildings and line up to take tours of monuments that are hundreds or even thousands of years old, such as the ruins of ancient Greece or the Pyramids, because despite everything they have seen, they endure to the present age. And it truly is impressive when you think that some of these places have been through multiple wars, severe storms, and abuse at the hand of the human race, and yet, there they stand.

In the light of the significance of their endurance, think of the Word of God and His promise that His mercy endures *forever.* Despite what we have thrown at it, despite the wars that rage in our lives, despite our failings, His mercy endures.

It is not about to run out.

But even more impressive than an old building, the mercy of God has stood and will continue to stand. How long will His mercy endure? It endures *forever,* which is longer than we can really grasp. His mercy will stand the test of time.

What a glimpse into the character of God! He is not an angry God. He is a good God rich in mercy.

So go ahead and read Psalm 136, and as you read this psalm or any other scripture you have read many times before, turn it over and over in your mind like this. Pick it apart—I guarantee God will show you something new each time you read it.

Did you really read it? Did you turn it over and look at it from different angles? Do you see that His mercy really *does* endure forever?

In a world where we call freak, destructive accidents of nature "acts of God," we are ignoring that God is *merciful.* You had mercy going to work today, coming home, on the way to church, when you flew to that business meeting. Every day of our lives there is mercy, mercy, mercy, again and again and again, that has carried us through things that you and I don't even know about.

So if you're looking for something to say thank you for, and you look around in your life and you can't find anything, look no further than this right here. You've got something to be thankful for today—His mercy endures forever!

Mercy Changed the Rules

I'd like to offer you a definition of mercy: Mercy is a whole new set of rules. The old rules said that if you mess up, you pay the price.

But then came mercy—a whole new set of rules. This is the heart of what I want to get across to you about mercy as a core component of God's character.

Often, I think, we say to ourselves, "I have sinned too big and I have sinned too loud this time."

But that's not what God's mercy says.

God's mercy endures. It has endured from the beginning, when, at the dawn of Creation, God looked into complete darkness and said, "Light *be,*" and it was. It was a challenge—God was making a statement.

And in His mercy, light overcame darkness and total emptiness in a world that was nothing. That's where it started, and it set a precedent God has maintained since then.

So if mercy can overcome this, it can overcome sin in our lives. Mercy can overcome doubt, failure, and faithlessness. It endures.

Psalm 145 tells us, "The Lord is merciful and compassionate, slow to get angry and filled with unfailing love" (verse 8, NLT).

The next verse says, "The Lord is good to all, and His tender mercies are over all His works" (NKJV).

Similarly, the entire 103rd Psalm is another testimony to God, and again look at the comparison between God's goodness and His anger: "The Lord is merciful and gracious, slow to anger, and abounding in mercy" (verse 8).

Does it say the Lord is vengeful and vindictive, quick to get angry and abounding in righteous wrath? No! It's not wrath and anger that endure; He's slow to anger but quick to mercy. Mercy defines God's character.

The psalm goes on to say, "He will not always accuse, nor will he harbor his anger forever; he does not treat us as our sins deserve or repay us according to our iniquities" (verses 9-10, NIV).

But what really strikes me about this verse comes earlier: David talks about God's benefits, saying He is the God who "forgives all your iniquities, who heals all your diseases, who redeems your life from destruction, who crowns you with lovingkindness and tender mercies" (verses 3-4).

God has crowned us, marked us. Is it His judgment that sits on our heads? Is it His righteous wrath? No! God crowned us with His lovingkindness and tender mercies.

A few verses later, the psalmist tells us that God made His ways known to Moses (verse 7). He called Moses and said, "Moses, I want you to speak for Me. I want you to stand and tell these people *I am*. I want you to stand and tell them who they're up against and reveal to them who I am and how I operate."

And in recounting God's faithfulness in this psalm throughout the life of Israel, this is what the psalmist focuses on—God's mercy.

Mercy Over Law

In Exodus 25, God is talking to Moses about building something—the "mercy seat." It sat on top of the Ark of the Covenant. The Ten Commandments were good, but they were *within* the Ark. But notice what was above the Law, covering everything.

Mercy.

Mercy changes the rules. We can try our best to keep every rule. We can try, in our flesh, to please God and do right. But we are not capable of it on our own.

And the rules say that when you break them, there is a price—death. "The wages of sin is death" (Romans 6:23).

Mercy didn't do away with the rules—God still gave them, and He still expected Moses to impart His commands to Israel and to us. He set high standards. But He put something higher than the rules—mercy.

•••

WE MUST RUN TO THE MERCY OF GOD.
IT CHANGES ALL THE RULES.

•••

I like to relate it to people in terms of parents raising their children. Personally, I believe we have way too many hands-off parents. We've got way too many people observing and saying, "Well, they'll learn for themselves. You've got to let them try it." Proverbs tells us, "Train up a child in the way he should go, and when he is old he will not depart from it" (Proverbs 22:6). Teach them the Word—teach them what the Word says about righteousness.

But most parents know that discipline without mercy is just asking for rebellion. Parents must set standards for their children, but then they also have an opportunity to illustrate the mercy of the heavenly Father. They can show them there is nothing their children must hide from them and that when they mess up they can run to their parents, rather than from them.

We can teach our children to run to mercy, but in doing so we are not doing anything more than God has illustrated for us. Hebrews tells us, "Let us therefore come boldly to the throne of grace." Why? "That we may obtain mercy and find grace to help in time of need" (Hebrews 4:16).

We must run to the mercy of God. It changes all the rules. Let's obtain mercy and grace together as we explore God's desire for us to experience His mercy.

Chapter Six

MERCY ME

Jesus believed in mercy; His ministry was steeped in it. And remember, Jesus said that He had not come to abolish the Law but to fulfill it (Matthew 5:17).

Jesus quoted this out of the book of Hosea twice in His ministry. Religious people were asking Him why He sat with sinners and tax collectors, and Jesus told them they needed to study the Bible better. "But go and learn what this means," He told them, "I desire mercy and not sacrifice" (Matthew 9:13). Later in His ministry, Jesus again told the hardhearted religious leaders how far they had missed God's character when they harassed Him for healing on the Sabbath (Matthew 12:7).

Jesus was trying to get a thought across to them: "I didn't come to save the righteous. I came to save the sinners. I'm changing all the rules. I'm changing what you thought was right."

Nowhere is Jesus' changing of the rules more evident than the sermon we call the Beatitudes. Particularly in Matthew 5 and Luke 6, Jesus' preaching is changing all the rules—in the same message He delivered where He tells them He hasn't come to abolish the Law.

Listen how He introduces a new way of thinking:

> You have heard that it was said, "You shall love your neighbor and hate your enemy." But I say to you, love your enemies, bless those who curse you, do good to those who hate you, and pray for those who spitefully use you and persecute you, that you may be sons of your Father in heaven; for He makes His sun rise on the evil and on the good, and sends rain on the just and on the unjust (Matthew 5:43-45).

Read that last part again, because it's important to realize that Jesus wasn't really saying anything new: He was revealing His Father's nature and character. Read how He sums it up in this line from Luke 6, which relates the same sermon: "Therefore be merciful, just as your Father also is merciful" (verse 36).

He was changing all their rules. He was teaching the mercy of God.

Like the hardhearted religious leaders, we have gotten it in our heads that God has to be appeased through sacrifice when we can't keep the Law—that He's just looking for a chance to smash us.

In Micah 6:7, we read, "Will the Lord be pleased with thousands of rams, ten thousand rivers of oil? Shall I give my firstborn for my transgression, the fruit of my body for the sin of my soul?"

He thought he understood the rules—failure required sacrifice. Like Micah, we've got it in our thinking that if we just keep sacrificing we'll please God. If we just keep trying to do what's right, if we just keep trying and trying and trying...

But look what God shows him in the next verse: "He has shown you, O man, what is good; and what does the Lord require of you but to do justly, to love mercy, and to walk humbly with your God?" (verse 8).

God was telling him then that He wanted to change the rules, that He desired mercy, not sacrifice. This is the revelation of a God who's not interested in appeasement and who isn't looking for sacrifice.

In fact, remember our definition of mercy—a whole new set of rules. The rules say that sin requires a payment: our lives. And Micah knew this; he was ready to do whatever God asked of him—he was ready to offer his firstborn!

•••

GOD WAS TELLING HIM THEN THAT HE WANTED TO CHANGE THE RULES, THAT HE DESIRED MERCY, NOT SACRIFICE.

•••

But God changed all the rules with Jesus. He gave *His* firstborn for our transgressions. The ultimate act of the ultimate Merciful One—Jesus, fulfilling the Law (the price) *and* revealing in flesh the mercy of God.

God is saying to us, "Here is the old rule: You mess up, you pay the price. But here is the new rule: You messed up, *I* paid the price." He is telling us, "Yeah, you messed up. Yeah, you blew it. But this is what we're going to do. We've got a new deal today. My firstborn for the transgression of your soul. I'll pay the price for what you did wrong, and if you're looking for a name for that, it's called mercy. And I want you to love it." He is more satisfied when we do justly, love mercy, and walk humbly with our God.

Humility

You might think this last part of Micah 6:8—walk humbly—is
odd. But I assure you it is not. Consider the nature of our rebellion as a race—we wanted to do it ourselves. We wanted what
God had. We are children wanting our own way, and it can actually keep us from God's mercy.

So how do we walk humbly? We simply accept reality. The reality is that all God has given to us through Jesus was not based on
what we deserved or what we did to earn it.

Despite what you might think, you don't have to try to be humble. Humility is you taking your part in the conversation between
grace and faith. Grace is God handing you a gift and saying,
"Hey, I got you something." Faith is you reaching out to receive it
and saying, "Thank You. I love it. It's exactly what I needed!"

...

HUMILITY IS YOU TAKING YOUR
PART IN THE CONVERSATION
BETWEEN GRACE AND FAITH.

...

So grace is God saying, "I noticed your robe was like filthy
rags so I got you this new white one. It even looks just like
Mine!" Faith is you saying, "Thank You! It fits perfectly!" This
is reality—there is nothing for you or me to boast about, there
is nothing to be proud of other than God and His free gift.
That is humility.

Take a look at Ephesians 2:1-5:

> As for you, you were dead in your transgressions and sins,
> in which you used to live when you followed the ways of
> this world and of the ruler of the kingdom of the air, the
> spirit who is now at work in those who are disobedient.

All of us also lived among them at one time, gratifying
the cravings of our sinful nature and following its desires
and thoughts. Like the rest, we were by nature objects of
wrath. But because of his great love for us, God, who is
rich in mercy, made us alive with Christ even when we
were dead in transgressions—it is by grace you have been
saved (NIV).

There was nothing different about you or me. Before God came
on the scene, we were just another nameless face in the crowd. We
lived by what came naturally to us—we followed our flesh, just
like everyone else. We were in darkness, dead in our trespasses.

But then came mercy.

Mercy found you in that crowd and called you by name. He
changed the rules. Now there's something different about you.
You called on mercy, and mercy came to you and separated you
from the crowd. And now you stand not with just your name. You
stand with His Name—Jesus.

Recognizing Mercy

I want to be quick to realize God's mercy—I want to see Him
moving in my life and the lives of others quickly, because I know
Him and that His character *is* mercy.

Really, we need go no further than the life and ministry of Jesus
for our example. What did the sick cry out to Him? "Jesus, son of
David, have mercy on me." Some would try to keep these people
quiet, but Jesus found the sick and healed them. And the healing
power of God flowed straight out of that mercy, just as salvation
flows from mercy.

A casual thought about this might say that without Jesus on
planet Earth for us to emulate today, it may be hard to look to

His example for mercy. But actually it's *because* of mercy He isn't here on this planet anymore.

Jesus sent the Holy Spirit, the Comforter—He said it's actually *better* this way! With the Holy Spirit's witness within us, I believe that we can learn to see God's mercy operating in our lives and in the lives of others before He has to knock on our door with a name tag on.

•••

TODAY, YOU AND I, WE ARE MERCY.

•••

We'll get more into the Holy Spirit's role later in the book, but for now I'd like to give you two ways of recognizing God's mercy. These aren't complicated action steps, but I believe they will help you know and understand the character of God embodied by His mercy.

The first step you can take to recognizing God's mercy in your life is to simply show mercy yourself. Going back to Matthew 5, Jesus tells us, "Blessed are the merciful." Why? "For they shall obtain mercy" (verse 7). Simple, right? You've received mercy—now it's time to show it.

I challenge you to seek out people in your life to whom you can show mercy—a change of the rules. When I preach about this, I hand out name tags that say, "Hello. My name is _____" and I have the people fill it out: MERCY.

Jesus was mercy to a fallen earth that deserved death, and He showed us all that God was changing the rules. He is inside us.

Today, you and I, *we* are Mercy.

Jesus tells an amazing story about mercy that's as relevant today as it was two thousand years ago. It was a parable about a man who owed a king multiple lifetimes of money. And he went before the king and fell down and pleaded with him. "Be patient with me. I'll pay it all back." And the king had compassion on him. (Here's your foreign language lesson for the day: All throughout the Word of God you find that *compassion* and *mercy* are the same word. You can look them up. They're exactly the same.)

But then Jesus contrasted this act of mercy with what can happen among us so easily. That servant, so recently forgiven a massive debt, goes and demands payment of a trifling debt from a fellow servant. The guy maybe owed him for lunch one day or something, yet the forgiven servant didn't really understand his king's character of mercy.

He demands payment, and the guy responds in a familiar way, "Be patient with me. I'll pay it all back." These were the very same words this man now demanding payment had himself spoken earlier, pleading with the king. So the servant who was so recently forgiven has that servant thrown into prison until he could pay the debt.

The king hears about it and isn't too happy with this—in fact, it's not pretty. When he found this out, he summoned his servant to come before him and said, "'You evil servant! I forgave you that tremendous debt because you pleaded with me. Shouldn't you have mercy on your fellow servant, just as I had mercy on you?' Then the angry king sent the man to prison to be tortured until he had paid his entire debt" (Matthew 18:32-34, NLT).

That is pretty sobering. But not near as sobering as Jesus' statement following this parable.

"That's what my heavenly Father will do to you if you refuse to forgive your brothers and sisters from your heart" (verse 35, NLT).

Whoa! God is going to throw us in prison and have us tortured if we don't show mercy and forgive?! I believe the truth is deeper than just that. Jesus is communicating that His Father cannot forgive us if we don't forgive others. And when we are outside of the mercy and forgiveness of the Father, we are left with harboring that unforgiveness. This unforgiveness will quite literally keep our souls in a prison of bitterness, tortured by the memory of how someone has done us wrong.

But when we truly accept the mercy of God toward us for all the ways we've missed it, our "new" natural response is to forgive and extend that same mercy toward others. It may not feel like a natural response at first, but when we stop and realize the many times mercy has been extended to us, forgiving others becomes the only reasonable response. There is power in the act of forgiveness. In the same way, unforgiveness can have power over an individual who refuses to forgive others.

Simply put, unforgiveness is allowing the past to rule the present and ruin the future. Write that down.

Grudge Holder or Mercy Carrier?

I'll tell you what—you can hold on to that bitterness and resentment toward a parent, friend, boss, or whomever, on one condition: If you seek the Lord and find out the blood of Jesus doesn't cover that sin toward you, you're totally justified. You're totally off the hook to forgive if you go before God regarding the way you've been hurt and He says to you, "They did what?! Jesus, did You hear that? I've never seen someone so wrongly treated. You poor thing. You have every right to be mad. There is not enough power in the blood of My Son to cover that one."

If that is His response, then I say stay mad. But if you sincerely go to God with this hurt, I think you are going to find that the precious blood of Jesus covers a multitude of sins. You are going to see that His mercy has been extended to you time and time again, and if you truly want to be a carrier of His divine nature then mercy must be your response, too.

...

BIG OR LITTLE,
FIND SOMEONE SOMEWHERE TO FORGIVE.

...

God has shown His character by showing mercy to us. We, in turn, show mercy to those around us, giving Him an opportunity to show His character to them.

Find someone to forgive. Big or little, find someone somewhere to forgive. Find someone who deserves their just deserts, but instead show this person how Jesus changed the rules. Show this person mercy.

I guarantee it will rock your proverbial world, and God will show you marvelous things about Himself as you do this.

Here's a thought for you: Wouldn't it be amazing if you weren't just a person who showed mercy—wouldn't it be a miracle if you literally left an atmosphere of mercy in your wake?

Let me explain that. I was on the way home one night and meditating on Psalm 23:6—"Surely goodness and mercy shall follow me all the days of my life." I was doing that trick I told you about earlier, thinking about each individual word, and it occurred to me to wonder about the word *follow*. What's it mean that goodness and mercy would *follow* me?

I felt like God responded by reminding me of this: *What did I tell Moses when he wanted to see Me? Moses asked to see My glory.* God put Moses under the rock and He hid him. God let Moses watch His back—so he wouldn't *die*. *What did I show him?* God prompted. Goodness—God showed Moses His goodness, and it left him changed, glowing!

Goodness follows Him. I don't think it's a stretch to say that goodness and mercy followed God.

Does goodness and mercy follow you? What happens after you leave a place? What goes on in the lives of people? What goes on in their workloads or in their own personal lives or their own struggles with this or that? What happens in the lives of others when you leave their presence?

• • •

So THE No. 1 WAY To BECOME FAMILIAR
WITH THE CHARACTER OF GOD
IN OUR LIFE IS SHOWING MERCY.

• • •

What if goodness and mercy followed you as they do God? What if you left people in your wake changed by having seen God's mercy? I believe we can have that effect in Jesus' Name!

So the No. 1 way to begin to become familiar with the character of God in our life is showing mercy.

But it will never happen until we have revelation that mercy has been shown to us. God changed the rules, and mercy found us in the crowd. He changed the rules for us! The extent of that must really sink in—the fact that it's not a one-time deal and that mercy has *endured* in your life. It has endured your failures again and again.

You must get that in order to go on to the second step.

Look for It

The second way we begin to recognize God in our lives is to think often of His mercy.

I'm blessed to be married to an absolutely wonderful, godly woman. However, Sarah Hart Pearsons is much more than my wife. She is a constant reminder of the mercy of God toward me.

I had already decided, before I ever met her, that if God was going to bring someone into my life and give me the opportunity to be a husband that she was going to be a demonstration of His mercy and goodness toward me.

One day in October I saw a picture of my cousin and a friend of hers. To make a long, amazing, make-you-believe-in-God story short, I met Sarah, the friend in the picture, six months later. When I met her, I heard God speaking softly on the inside, saying, *Jeremy, I want you to meet My mercy on your life.*

That was it for me! We were married six months after that.

I did not meet Sarah because I deserved her or because of something I did for God. It was pure, total mercy. It's not hard for me to look for the mercy of God. Every morning, I wake up next to an example of God's mercy—it's amazing, and it keeps God's enduring mercy in front of my eyes daily.

There are people in your life who are there because God is merciful toward you. It may be the very person you are struggling to get along with, like that boss you wish you didn't have.

Ask the Lord to open the eyes of your heart so that you can see His unending mercy toward you. You may be surprised to see His mercy demonstrated in some unexpected places. But when you do begin to recognize His mercy when you see it, don't let it stop there. We should think often of how wonderfully blessed we are to have such an outward demonstration of the nature of God put on display for us to see.

When you make much of the mercy of God, it opens the door to receive more than you ever have before. It's as though God says, "Oh you like that, huh? Well, what about this?" Then you see something or someone in a way that you never have before, and you realize that every good and perfect gift is from God. You realize that the gift has nothing to do with what you actually deserve but comes only because He is so good and merciful toward those who worship Him.

Recognize It

So be merciful—that's the first step. The second step is easy for me; think of His mercy all the time. When you think often of His mercy toward you, it will make showing His mercy toward others that much easier. His mercy truly has endured, it will continue to endure, and it will endure forever! There is no end to His mercy, and it's so important that we begin to grasp this attribute of His character.

I want to get to know God better and better, to recognize Him in my life when He is moving subtly and slightly. I believe we can do this—I believe that we can know God well enough to spot His move, to know His still, small voice when it first shows up in our lives.

We must get to know Him—learn what He's like. It's all in His Word, and here we have made a beginning.

He is good, and His mercy endures forever.

God is MERCY.

Mercy is a funny thing though. It is best understood when you grasp whom it came from and what place of authority they hold. In God, there is no higher rank. There is no greater authority.

So let's look at these elements of God together in the next section.

SECTION III

MOST HIGH

Chapter Seven

OVER AND UNDER

Is it possible that God can be in the middle of our lives—right here among us, sitting next to us—without us knowing it? I believe it is. We can claim to have a relationship with Him, without actually knowing Him very well at all. Sadly, I believe this is happening every day.

But He wants us to know Him. He is a mystery hidden *for* us. Not *from* us.

The Word of God is amazing because, through human vessels, God has used it to reveal Himself to us. Everything He said, everything He's done, every promise He's made and fulfilled within the Word is a testimony to His character. Any concept we have of faith, hope, love, faithfulness, or mercy derives directly from our Father.

We must ask Him to open our hearts and minds, to open our eyes, and to motivate and inspire us to a closer relationship with Him. We need Him to reveal His character to us—all so we can know Him better and see His involvement in our lives.

...

HE IS A MYSTERY HIDDEN FOR US.
NOT FROM US.

...

Getting to know Him better is the only way that we are ever going to get past the point where God has no choice but to knock on our doors and show up wearing a name tag: "Hello. My name is God." My underlying question here is, "Would you know Him if you saw Him?"

You can get to know Him well enough to hear His still, small voice within you.

I believe I am a part of a generation that is not easily fooled. I think of the story where a man would show up in a town with a bottle of his "Wonder Drug" and claim that for only a few dollars he could heal all of what ails the body and soul. Of course, many of these turned out to be hucksters and charlatans looking to dupe some simple minds out of their hard-earned money.

The thought of someone trying that today is preposterous. Today, if you want to fool someone into buying your product, you'd better be ready to support it with a multimillion-dollar ad campaign and total market saturation. But I think most of our generation is saying, "We know too much. We've seen too much. You can't fool us. You say your product works? Prove it!" In some ways, this is good. As a result we live in a generation that is less likely to believe a lie.

But the "prove it to me" philosophy doesn't fly when you're talking to God. He has offered proof over and over throughout the ages, and He is looking for those who will find Him in His Word and love the Truth they find there.

Perhaps you are a thinker, analyzer, or even a critic of the world around you. I challenge you to not let that tendency stand between you and trusting Him with all your heart—between you and having faith.

But I don't encourage you to do this because I'm afraid that the Word can't hold up to your analytical mind. Over the centuries, far superior minds to ours have held the Bible up against the harshest criticism—and time and again it has proven itself.

In fact, I invite you to dig and see just how deep you can go. But as you look, look through the eyes of faith, not doubt and skepticism. When you search with a pure heart, you will find exactly what you are looking for.

Most people want to see before they believe. But if you want to see God, He requires you to believe first.

We looked at the story of Jesus and the woman at the well in which He engaged her in a conversation that could have led her to know Him. But she failed to pick up on where He was trying to take her. The Messiah, for whom she claimed to be looking, was sitting there with her, and she didn't know. It wasn't until He finally revealed Himself obviously that she understood to whom she was speaking, but the entire time, He was seeking one thing from her. It's the same thing He seeks from us today:

Belief.

In the previous section, we took a look at God's mercy— a world-changing concept for some people who have always thought that God was a ticked-off, vindictive deity. We learned that instead of His wrath and anger enduring, it's His mercy that endures forever. It's His mercy that defines Him. We learned that no matter what we throw at it, no matter how bad it gets, His mercy endures *forever.*

I left you with two assignments: being merciful and always looking for God's mercy in your life. When I began to do this, I started seeing so much in my life that was obviously God's mercy in operation.

I want to build on the understanding that God is good and merciful. And remember, what is mercy? It's God changing all the rules. Mercy is God making everything new—we deserved judgment, but instead Mercy came to earth. Simultaneously, Mercy fulfilled the Law and yet changed all the rules.

So with that understanding of God beginning to dawn, let's move on and take a look at another component of God I want you to see—His place of authority.

To begin, I want to take a look at a couple of key scriptures.

In Mark we read,

> The people were amazed at his teaching, because he taught them as one who had authority, not as the teachers of the law…. The people were all so amazed that they asked each other, "What is this? A new teaching—and with authority! He even gives orders to evil spirits and they obey him" (Mark 1: 22, 27, NIV).

This didn't go unnoticed. Jesus was stepping on some toes. Reading on, it says, "Now when He came into the temple, the chief priests and the elders of the people confronted Him as He was teaching, and said, 'By what authority are You doing these things? And who gave You this authority?'" (verse 23).

Matthew 7:28-29 echoes these other two: "When Jesus had finished these sayings [the Sermon on the Mount], the crowds were *astonished* and overwhelmed with *bewildered wonder* at His teaching, for He was teaching as One Who had [and was] authority, and not as [did] the scribes" (AMP).

In order to understand why they were "astonished and overwhelmed with bewildered wonder," you have to understand how Jewish rabbis taught. The entire basis for a rabbi's teaching was the one under whom he studied. When they taught, they said something like, "Well, this is my opinion based on Rabbi Soand-So's opinion, based on what he thought about this scripture, which is based on what his teacher, Rabbi Such-and-Such, said about that." This isn't necessarily a wrong way to learn and teach, but it's definitely not the way Jesus taught. And the difference was obvious to everyone who heard it.

So when it says they were astonished that He taught them with authority, unlike the scribes and Pharisees, it's because Jesus introduced something entirely new to these people when He began changing all the rules. They were preoccupied with rules—with the Law and all the additions they made to it. They had been missing God's mercy and goodness, and now that Jesus was beginning to show them the Father, it simply astonished and amazed them.

••••

> I BELIEVE THEY MISSED HIM BECAUSE THEY COULD NOT RECOGNIZE HIS PLACE OF AUTHORITY.

••••

Jesus' teaching was not based on any rabbi's—it was entirely new to these people. This was no longer a man teaching based on what somebody else had said about something; Jesus began revealing God's mercy and said, "I don't say anything unless it comes from My Father."

And this shows how thoroughly it took them by surprise: These people, who saw Him perform miracles by healing the sick and raising the dead and heard Him say things like, "If you do what I say, you'll have everlasting life," *didn't get it.* They were filled with wonder.

When it says they were filled with amazed wonder, it isn't really complimentary; they were saying, "Huh—look at that. Isn't that interesting? Wonder where he picked that up…"

I believe they missed Him for one main reason: They could not recognize *His place of authority.*

Think they're alone in this, that this doesn't happen anymore? Don't be so sure.

So What Now?

In praying about what God was showing me about knowing Him better, I spent a lot of time asking Him what was next— what came after mercy. And I felt like God impressed on me, *My people are not quick enough to recognize My place of authority.*

The connection between knowing Him and recognizing His place of authority may not at first be apparent, but think of this: We live in a world spiraling away from the values of the Bible. Western society in particular has adopted situational ethics as a standard; we talk about concepts like moral relativism and tolerance in place of the concrete standards in the Word. Everything is relative—what works for me may not work for you, and who are you to judge me and enforce your "opinion" on my life?

We are losing an ability to acknowledge that God created standards and revealed them to us in His Word—standards that are absolutes and that don't change with the passing of time or the evolution of society.

Don't see how this affects our ability to know God? Let's use mercy as the foundation, and I will show you how understanding and recognizing God's authority can open your eyes to knowing Him more than you have before. I will show you how they go hand in hand—knowing God, seeing Him in your life, and acknowledging His authority are intimately linked.

Over and Under

The religious leaders of His day missed every part of Jesus' ministry because they could not connect Him with His place of authority. Think of it: These men and women were eyewitnesses of the life and ministry of Jesus Christ, and they missed the whole thing! The same is true today: *My people are not quick enough to recognize My place of authority.*

So we've established it is possible to be face to face with Jesus and not know Him—not recognize Him—and failing to recognize His place of authority is one of the ways in which we miss Him.

But not everyone in Jesus' day missed His authority.

In Matthew 8:5, we read of a Roman centurion coming to Jesus because his servant is paralyzed and suffering. Jesus responds to this man's plea for help by saying He will come heal the man's servant. And none of this is terribly unusual; the gospels are full of people coming to Jesus for healing. So while this story is not uncommon in Jesus' life, what happens next is.

The Roman officer responds to Jesus,

> Lord, I am not worthy that You should come under my roof. But only speak a word, and my servant will be healed. For I also am a man under authority, having soldiers under me. And I say to this one, "Go," and he goes; and to another, "Come," and he comes; and to my servant, "Do this," and he does it (verses 8-9).

In the light of the religious leaders totally missing His place of authority, a *gentile*—a non-Jew—recognizing it is truly amazing. We've read about others being astonished at Jesus, but now He is the one being amazed. "When Jesus heard it, He marveled, and said to those who followed, 'Assuredly, I say to you, I have not found such great faith, not even in Israel!'" (verse 10).

Something different just happened. Something unique. Something isolated in Jesus' life and ministry that had not ever taken place up to this point. Jesus had gone with this one, gone with that one, gone to minister here, gone to perform a miracle there. But never had anyone responded like this. It literally stopped Jesus in His tracks. He was headed to the centurion's house, but when he said this, Jesus had to stop and marvel at it.

The religious leaders *marveled* in unbelief. Jesus *marveled* at this man's faith.

...

JESUS HAD NEVER SEEN
ANYTHING LIKE THIS MAN'S FAITH
AND HIS UNDERSTANDING OF
AUTHORITY—OVER AND UNDER.

...

Most of us understand a desire for approval from our parents. Even people with a bad upbringing often have a deep desire to hear, "Way to go. Good job." Pretty much everyone wants approval from those in authority over us.

But let's progress beyond human approval for a second and think about what it would be like to have that from God, what it would be like to have that kind of approval from Jesus Himself. What would it be like for you or me to do or say something that caused Jesus to stop and say, "I have never seen anything like this before"?

Because that's exactly what He did with this centurion. Just a few verses before, you have religious people completely missing it—people who claimed to know something about God and thought they were looking for the Messiah. But they missed the whole ministry of Jesus because they didn't recognize His authority. And then here's a man who understands Jesus' authority completely, and he's a gentile—even more, he's an officer in an oppressive regime!

Jesus had never seen anything like this man's faith and his understanding of authority—over and under.

In fact, I believe it was the centurion's understanding of authority—both being over other people and also under others' authority—that produced his faith in Jesus. He understood the concept of name and rank and this idea of a place of authority.

And if you and I ever begin to understand how this works—ever begin to put God in this place of authority—we will understand that not only *can* He, not only is He *able,* but He is *willing* to impact our lives, just as Jesus was. There is something about realizing that the God of the universe—the Creator of heaven and earth, the One who bears this name, the One who carries this rank—is the author of all goodness and mercy that produces faith in you. When you understand that all of His omnipotent authority is founded on mercy, you will run to Him instead of from Him when you mess up.

He is the only one with authority to say, "I forgive you. Now let's go on."

Mercy operates because of authority, because to extend mercy, you have to come from a place of authority. If I am merciful to someone, it means that in some way that person owed me something. I have authority to give mercy or withhold it—my call, my decision, my authority.

We must recognize His place of authority over us so we can accept His mercy. So let's take a closer look at His place of authority…

Name and Rank

We will define authority for our purposes as name and rank. Those in the army or another branch of the armed forces understand rank, as the centurion did. Most of us understand the concept pretty well; generals run the show, they've got colonels and majors and captains and lieutenants under them. The same goes for the enlisted ranks—everyone knows who is over him and who is under him because of rank.

Let's leave it at that for now and go on to God's name. What is His name? Contrary to popular belief, His name is not actually just "God." God is something we English-speaking people got from the old German word "gott," which deals with the *rank* of a deity. So if His name isn't God, then what is it?

Well, how did He introduce Himself to Moses? Moses was out watching sheep on a mountainside, and God introduced Himself in a burning bush. He began to disclose to Moses the call of destiny on his life—delivering His people from bondage.

So Moses, ever the practical one, asks, "Who do I say sent me?"

And God comes back with, "Tell them *I Am* sent you." That's the first way He introduced Himself to Moses.

"Hello, my name is God," He was telling Moses. "I *am*. I am that I am. I am Alpha. I am Omega. I am the beginning; I am the end; and I am everything in between. I am your Provider. I am your Healer. I am your Breakthrough. I am your Defense. I am your Father. I am your God. This is who I am."

And then He sent His Son, who quotes from Isaiah:

> The Spirit of the Lord is on me, because he has anointed me to preach good news to the poor. He has sent me to proclaim freedom for the prisoners and recovery of sight for the blind, to release the oppressed, to proclaim the year of the Lord's favor (Luke 4:18-19, NIV).

He came and said, "I am the Christ, the Anointed One. I am the One who has come to remove burdens. I am the One who has come to destroy yokes. I am the anointing made flesh, the Word of God made flesh. I am the One who restores your relationship with God. I am the Morning Star, the firstborn from the dead. I am your Advocate with the Father. I am Savior, Brother, Friend." This is His name.

And He in turn sends the Holy Spirit. "I am the Comforter. I am the Standby. I am the Spirit of Truth. I am your Teacher, and I am the one who convicts of sin and draws men to God. I am your Helper."

I am. *I Am.* I AM. This is the name of God, but "I Am" is not just a name. It is a name with a promise in it. It is a name that is not only heard, it is seen. It is witnessed. It is a name that demonstrates itself in power.

But we are not just studying His name. We are learning the reputation behind the name.

...

THERE IS NONE HIGHER THAN OUR GOD.
THERE IS NO HIGHER PLACE OF AUTHORITY.
THERE IS NO HIGHER RANK.
THERE IS NO HIGHER NAME.

...

Most High

All throughout the Word of God, He discloses His name to us.
We could spend weeks and months just talking about the name
of God—something so sacred and holy that the Israelites thought
it was unspeakable. His is a name so weighty, so full of glory that
human lips didn't dare utter it.

Now *that's* a name with authority.

Let's get back to rank for a moment. Let's talk about where
He fits in the chain of command. Over and over again, the Bible
gives God His place. I won't even try to cover them all, but here's
just a taste: Psalm 7:17 says, "I will praise the Lord according to
His righteousness, and will sing praise to the name of the Lord
Most High."

Psalm 21:7 says, "For the king trusts in the Lord, and through
the mercy of the *Most High* he shall not be moved."

Psalm 47:2 says, "For the Lord *Most High* is awesome; He is a
great King over all the earth."

Do you see a pattern yet? We could go on and on like this—
Most High, Most High, Most High.

When you begin to talk and discuss the name and rank of God,
is there any higher than Most High? Who is higher than most
high? No one. What is better than most high? Nothing. That's
it—He is Most High.

Now if you really stop and think about it, is there even a close
second? Is there even one that compares to the *most?* We don't

serve a God who has accomplished some things. You and I don't worship the Lord over this and that and maybe one or two other things. We worship *the* Most High. There is none higher than our God. There is no higher place of authority. There is no higher rank. There is no higher name. This is the Lord Most High.

We've got to begin to be quicker to recognize this—quicker to give God His place of authority, quicker to recognize who He is and His name and His rank. Let's see how exactly we do that.

Chapter Eight

BECAUSE I SAID SO

Every parent with young children learning to ask questions knows about the "why" conversation. A parent will say to his or her small child, "Turn the TV off, it's time for dinner."

And the little one says in return, "Why?"

And with great patience the parent replies, "Because it's time to eat, and you need to eat to grow big and strong."

"But why?"

"Because Mommy made us a good dinner and she doesn't want it to get cold, OK?"

"But why?"

And this could go on and on because Mommy or Daddy is trying to communicate with a 3-year-old to help the little one understand and comprehend so that he or she will finally obey his instruction. But if you have ever been involved in this kind of conversation, then you know quite well that there is an answer coming. It is an answer that will put a permanent end to this discussion.

And what is that answer? "Because I said so!"

You can explain all kinds of things, but you can only go so far with a 3-year-old. Eventually, you reach a point where all the understanding they need is *because you said so*. Cars in the street, big ugly dogs, and a host of other things don't wait for explanation time—obedience because you said so can be vital.

For some reason, I think Momma says it best. And what is she doing when she says that? She is saying, "Listen. You have to obey because I am who I am. My name is Momma. My rank is Momma. You don't talk back to this name. You don't talk back to this rank. You obey." Why? "Because I said so."

And all the mommas said, "Amen."

Unfortunately, a firm understanding of this kind of authority isn't as common today as it once was. In an effort to be sensitive—or simply out of apathy or error—parents have largely abdicated their position of authority in their children's lives.

We don't have the same level of respect for Momma and Daddy as perhaps we once did. Is it any wonder that we can miss recognizing the authority of the Most High in our lives?

So how do we begin to recognize authority? We've talked about mercy—being merciful and being quick to recognize mercy in our lives. How do we begin to be quick to recognize authority?

Obey it.

It doesn't get much simpler than that. Obey. We need to quit stalling, quit demanding answers, and simply learn to obey *because He said so*.

Help With Authority

For many of us, obedience itself is less than easy. We may have had people in authority abuse it or just be fiercely independent. Whatever the case, there are many of us for whom learning to be obedient is a challenge.

Praise God, He hasn't left us alone to figure it out on our own. Mercy is in operation even in this: He gave us the Holy Spirit.

John 16:13 says, "However, when He, the Spirit of truth, has come, He will guide you into all truth; for He will not speak on His own authority, but whatever He hears He will speak; and He will tell you things to come."

The Holy Spirit understands authority because He operates in God's authority. And it's important that He teach us this, because when we begin to recognize God's place of authority, obedience is no longer optional—when we truly understand what His authority means, it changes how we handle things.

•••

WE'RE ACCOUNTABLE WHEN WE
ACCEPT THE HOLY SPIRIT'S ROLE
IN SHOWING US GOD'S AUTHORITY.

•••

Amazingly, God still always gives us a choice—obey or disobey. He gives us choices, but then He tells us which one is best. Deuteronomy 30:19 says, "I have set before you life and death, blessing and cursing; *therefore choose life,* that both you and your descendants may live."

We've got choices, but there are some that are better than others. And through the Holy Spirit, we can know which one we should take. The effect is that when you really know what's laid before you—blessing or cursing, life or death—the choice is clear.

Obedience is no longer optional because when the Spirit of the Lord is leading us, we realize that God's direction is a command coming directly from the Most High. We reach a new level of accountability when we accept the Holy Spirit's role in showing us God's authority.

When Jesus says the Holy Spirit will "guide" us in John 16:13, the wording there is perhaps more accurately translated that the Holy Spirit is like a tour guide—someone who is completely familiar with every twist and turn in the path, every obstacle, every danger. It paints the picture of someone who has been there and back again—and again, and again.

You have the ultimate tour guide living in you, and now He's come alongside you, saying, "Ah, listen. I've been where you're going. I've been there. Just up ahead there's a hole in this road that you're going to want to avoid. And over there's a dark place, but if you'll listen to Me, I'll lead you right around it."

If you'll listen, if you will obey the command from the Most High, you will stay in the light. You will avoid the injuring, damaging traps of life. You will be where He wants you to be, when He wants you to be there.

Can you see how important it is to recognize His place of authority?

Be Quick to Obey

We don't have to forge ahead in recognizing God's authority on our own; we have help in the form of the Holy Spirit. Yet a tremendous amount of obedience is simply *doing* what God asks of us—quickly and without the "why" conversation as though we were 3-year-olds.

My wife and I are friends with a couple that has four children. I spend a lot of time with the father of this family, and his explanation of this concept was the best I have heard.

When he gives an instruction to his kids, he doesn't necessarily mind if they ask, "why," as long as they are asking while they are on their way to obedience. In other words, they are not demanding to know why *before* they become willing to obey. That would be disrespect and rebellion.

If an explanation is necessary, then he is happy to as long as his kids have *already responded* in obedience to his instruction.

And yet all too often, we make our slow (or lack of) obedience *sound* spiritual. We say things like, "Well, you know, the Lord has been dealing with me for a while on that...." It sounds innocuous; it even sounds spiritual to us and perhaps others. But the truth is, if He has been dealing with you for some time, that means you didn't obey the first time He said it.

Being slow to obey can be every bit as bad as deciding to not obey, and this type of thinking must end if we are to really recognize God's authority.

This is one of the reasons we had to talk about mercy first—because all of us are guilty of putting off obedience to God. And in that, we have sinned against the Lord. Yes, that's right—*sinned.*

...

BEING SLOW TO OBEY CAN BE EVERY
BIT AS BAD AS DECIDING TO NOT OBEY.

...

Every single one of us is guilty of hearing something from God and putting it off. Every one of us has delayed obedience. Sometimes it's because we don't know Him well enough to recognize His voice; other times, it's because we're stubborn or lazy. But whatever the cause, it's still sin, pure and simple.

Just as a child needs to quickly obey, so too must we. Lives—our own and others—can hang in the balance. Jesus came to give life, but we must respond to Him out of obedience if you and I want to have and enjoy the life He came to give.

We must hear and obey the Spirit of God inside us for the sake of the people our lives touch. Obedience is *crucial*—and not grudging, slow obedience.

We must obey *because He said so.* But to hear and obey, we must know His still, small voice. We need to hear and respond before He has to knock on our door wearing His "God" name tag.

When we begin to be led by the Spirit and recognize God's authority, you and I should make the determination that as far as we are concerned, our obedience is no longer optional. Like Paul, we must understand that Mercy freed us from sin and death but made us a slave to Christ—but this is no slavery at all, because it's being a slave to life instead of death and blessing instead of cursing!

•••

MERCY MADE US SLAVES
TO LIFE INSTEAD OF DEATH!

•••

Agony

Let's stop and think for a moment why in the world we would not be quick to obey the leading of the Spirit of God inside us. We know He is good and that His plan for us is not evil. We know He is merciful and not a vengeful, vindictive God.

So why, then? What could possibly keep us from simply yielding?

Romans 8:14 says, "For as many as are led by the Spirit of God, these are sons of God." The answer is in that little word *led.* It is the Greek word *ago,* the root of the word we translate "agony."

This obedience thing—being led by the Spirit and recognizing God's authority—can literally be agonizing to the part of us that stays selfish, stubborn, and sinful, even after we're saved.

Paul called this part of us "the flesh." And he tells us that we must put it to death—crucify it. Hang it on the Cross and leave it there.

He says, "I have been crucified with Christ; it is no longer I who live, but Christ lives in me; and the life which I now live in the flesh I live by faith in the Son of God, who loved me and gave

Himself for me" (Galatians 2:20).

The flesh doesn't like being under authority. It doesn't like taking the Holy Spirit's direction instead of making up its own mind about what it wants to do.

Proverbs 3:5-8 says,

> Trust in the Lord with all your heart, and lean not on your own understanding; in all your ways acknowledge Him, and He shall direct your paths. Do not be wise in your own eyes; fear the Lord and depart from evil. It will be health to your flesh, and strength to your bones.

Notice it says nothing about the devil, evil people, or sin—nothing about all of the things that we claim are the downfall of our lives. It says trust in the Lord with all your heart, because the opposite is leaning on your own understanding. Notice what this verse calls "evil"—being wise in your own eyes. And that is humbling.

So what prevents us from seeing His place of authority? What is standing between you and immediate obedience?

Pride.

James, quoting Proverbs a few verses down from this, says, "God resists the proud, but gives grace to the humble" (James 4:6).

Why do we miss God? Why do we fail to follow His leading? What prevents us from recognizing God's place of authority?

•••

UNDERSTANDING HIS AUTHORITY PRODUCES TRUST IN GOD THAT ALLOWS HIM TO MOVE ON OUR BEHALF.

•••

Pride—we lean on our own understanding and are wise in our own eyes instead of acknowledging Him in all our ways.

Conversely, when we trust in the Lord and recognize His authority, we allow faith to grow in our hearts that makes Jesus stop and take notice. Understanding His authority produces trust in God that allows Him to move on our behalf.

But when you let the Spirit lead you like this, be prepared—it will agonize your flesh. It can even be agony on your natural way of thinking.

•••

YOU'VE GOT TO GET OUT OF WHAT YOU KNOW
AND INTO WHAT YOU TRUST.

•••

Just when you think you've got everything figured out, you see an instruction in His Word or hear the leading of the Spirit that for some reason just doesn't seem to make sense. Be very watchful here. Proverbs says that there is a way that seems right to a man but the end is death. I heard my grandfather say once that you've got to get out of what you know and into what you trust.

The crucifixion of the flesh is agony but it's absolutely worth it.

Pride

I'd like to take a quick look at an example from the Bible of how pride can foul up an otherwise marvelous walk with God. Most of you know of Job, a righteous man who lived during the Old Testament. A lot has been written about how he walked uprightly with the Lord. He did a lot of things really right, but there were a couple of things that he did and said really wrong.

Job suffered a great deal, and though he never cursed God, as his wife urged him, he did begin to question God.

He became prideful, thinking that he was smart enough to determine it hadn't profited him anything to be a righteous man because bad things still happened to him. He questioned God's authority.

Until finally God shows up in Job 38. It says, "Then the Lord answered Job from the whirlwind: 'Who is this that questions my wisdom with such ignorant words?'" (verses 1-2, NLT). God tells him to get ready—He's going to put him to the question:

> Where were you when I laid the foundations of the earth? Tell me, if you know so much. Who determined its dimensions and stretched out the surveying line? What supports its foundations, and who laid its cornerstone as the morning stars sang together and all the angels shouted for joy? (verses 4-7, NLT).

God goes on and on, asking Job in his pride who set boundaries on the sea, who commanded the morning to come, and who has seen the gates of death. He asks if Job has seen the storehouse of the snow, who creates the rain, and who directs the movement of the stars.

It goes on like this for three more chapters—God putting Job in his place. Just in chapter 38, God asks Job forty-one questions, and each is beyond his understanding. His only answer is, "I don't know."

God revealed His place of authority and majesty to Job.

If you think about these questions that He asked Job, they are questions that our children today ask us. "Where does rain come from?" "Where do snow and hail and clouds come from?" "What are clouds made out of?" We consider them such childish questions. But the moment this man rose up in pride and tried to exalt himself by questioning the righteousness and justice of God, God showed up and said, "Let me ask you a few simple questions, Job."

And Job's only answer is, "I don't know." God was forced to reveal His place of authority to Job. He had to. He had to show up and say, "This is My Name and this is My rank." This story ended with Job saying in chapter 42, "I have heard you with my ears but now my eyes have seen you. Therefore I repent."

When Job came face to face with the majesty of God, he fell to his knees and repented. Do you know what it means to repent? You may have a picture of you or someone else on their knees at the front of the church, crying loudly and shedding big tears. I know that has happened, and I'm sure many who cry are very sincere.

But repenting very simply means to change one's mind. In the same way, confessing simply means to say the same thing as someone else. When we repent before God, we are changing our minds from the way we used to think about something to the way He thinks about it. We are saying, "Your thoughts are higher than the thoughts I've been thinking. I'm coming up to Your way of thinking."

...

REPENTING VERY SIMPLY MEANS
TO CHANGE ONE'S MIND.

...

Confessing your sin is saying the same thing about sin that He says about it: "Your ways are higher than the ways I've been living, so I repent and come up to the way You would do it."

Repentance and confession can take place every day, and it doesn't have to be at the altar of a church, or to a priest or pastor. It can take place in your car, at the table, or any place the Spirit of God is being given room to move.

If you ever wonder what God's place of authority is, just read the last few chapters of Job, where God is expounding upon His majesty. Really read it and think about where your own place is, compared to that.

When you know your place under authority and you recognize God's place of authority over *all,* you have made a great step in being able to hear and obey the still, small voice with which He wants to direct our lives.

Now that we've started to take a look at God's place of authority, let's see how we fit in. Read on!

Chapter Nine

THE TRUTH ABOUT YOU

I spend a lot of my time telling people who they are *in Christ*. When you made Jesus the Lord of your life, He gave you a new identity. In Him you are a new creation. In Him you are the righteousness of God. In Him you are an overcomer and conqueror. In Him you are loved. That's who you are in Him, and we'll talk more about that later.

But what about who you are in you—without Him?

Pastor Keith Moore teaches a series I highly recommend on humility. He discusses what he calls four "In You" truths—who we are in ourselves. So let's talk about who we are in our smarts, in our strength, in our own accomplishments. What are we by ourselves, without God? Please be advised, this next part may sting a little.

The first In You truth is this: In yourself, you *are* nothing. Ouch!

Galatians 6:3 says, "For if anyone thinks himself to be something, when he is nothing, he deceives himself." The Greek word here for *nothing* is pretty simple: "no, not one thing." Some people think they are something because of what they've done or who they are, but this scripture paints pride in an unflattering light. Despite how well you think of yourself, alone, you are nothing.

So the first In You truth is that, in yourself, you are nothing. These are harsh, but hold on—it gets worse before it gets better.

The second In You truth: In yourself, you *know* nothing.

First Corinthians 8:2 says, "And if anyone thinks that he knows anything, he knows nothing...." No, not one thing.

"But I've been to school. I've gone to college. I've been educated. I've seen some things. I've done some things." No. You know nothing. Hold what little you think you know up to the majesty of God, and you discover that we know little to nothing—and it's closer to nothing. In yourself, you know nothing.

Second In You truth: You know nothing.

The third In You truth is that in yourself, you *have* nothing.

First Corinthians 4:7 asks, "What do you have that God hasn't given you? And if everything you have is from God, why boast as though it were not a gift?" (NLT).

The Bible tells us that every good and perfect gift comes from the Father. We need to make a big deal out of mercy and grace—any good thing that shows up in our lives we should attribute to God. We should be quick to say, "This was the goodness of God!" Anything you learn, anything you receive, anything that makes your life blessed—it came from God, and we need to give Him credit.

I know full well that if the grace of God lifted from me for one moment I would have a hard time knowing my name. I'm not sure we can draw our next breath without God's grace.

In You truth No. 3: Without Him, we have nothing.

And the fourth In You truth is that in yourself, you can *do* nothing.

John 15:5 says, "Yes, I am the vine; you are the branches. Those who remain in me, and I in them, will produce much fruit. For apart from me you can do nothing" (NLT).

"Well, you can do small things," some people argue. "You can do little things, and the big stuff is for God."

Absolutely not. You and I can do *nothing* on our own.

The fourth In You truth: You can do nothing.

In Christ

Now in case you are feeling a little depressed after reading that, let me cheer you up. You and I don't have to live life being nothing, knowing nothing, having nothing, and doing nothing. That's because we were never designed to live on our own.

When we trust in the Lord with all our heart *instead of* leaning on our own understanding, we place ourselves in His capable hands. His ability becomes our ability. His strength is our strength. His wisdom is our wisdom.

You *are* the righteousness of God *in Christ!* Never forget those two all-important words: *In Christ.*

You have an unction, an anointing, from the Holy One, and you *know* all things. Never be deceived into thinking that you know something that wasn't revealed to you by the Holy Spirit. He is listening to Jesus, and Jesus is only saying what He hears His Father say.

•••

HIS ABILITY BECOMES OUR ABILITY.
HIS STRENGTH IS OUR STRENGTH.
HIS WISDOM IS OUR WISDOM.

•••

God has supplied all your needs according to His riches in glory by Christ Jesus. Second Corinthians 9:8 tells us that in Him you *have* all sufficiency in all things that you may *have* an abundance for every good work.

You *can do* all things. On your own? No! Through Christ, who strengthens you.

Remember Humility

It's good to remember those four truths about ourselves—we are nothing, we know nothing, we have nothing, and we can do nothing. It's a real confidence booster. Remind yourself of these things from time to time.

If it weren't for God, we would stay nothing.

Never forget who you are in Him, and never forget who you are without Him. Never forget the authority you are under, but don't forget the authority and what God has placed you over, either.

Remember, one thing stands between you and recognizing God's place of authority—pride.

Recall the scripture we looked at in the section on mercy in Micah 6. God doesn't want thousands of rams as a sacrifice, and He doesn't want our firstborn child. He has told us what He wants of us, and that is that we do what is right, love mercy, and walk humbly with our God (verses 7-8).

Now, when I'm preaching about mercy, I hand out name tags and have people fill them out "Hello. My name is MERCY" and then go out and be merciful. When preaching on God's authority, it's a little different: We fill out the name tag, "Hello. My name is HUMILITY." I have people put it on—put on humility. This really isn't for the sake of the people who see them as much as for the sake of those wearing the tags.

It's a great reminder to them that as they walk out, they are to walk humbly before God. It reminds them to not let pride in and to give credit to God for everything that's good in their lives.

•••

I WANT To SHOW YOu HOW HUMILITY
UNLOCKS SOMETHING IN YOuR LIFE.

•••

I gave you two things you can do to recognize God's mercy on your life—being merciful, and looking for and recognizing God's mercy on your life. Similarly, I want to give you two things you can do to encourage recognition of God's authority in your life. The first involves remembering all we have just learned about humility.

The first thing you can do is humble yourself. Be humble. If you are "trying to be humble" then you have missed the whole point. Humility is not something you *try.* Humility is reality. It is recognizing that all good things come from Him and in turn giving Him all the praise and glory.

I want to show you in just a couple of scriptures how humility unlocks something in your life.

> In the same way, you younger men must accept the authority of the elders. And all of you, serve each other in humility, for "God opposes the proud but favors the humble." So humble yourselves under the mighty power of God, and at the right time he will lift you up in honor. Give all your worries and cares to God, for he cares about you. Stay alert! Watch out for your great enemy, the devil. He prowls around like a roaring lion, looking for someone to devour. Stand firm against him, and be strong in your faith. Remember that your Christian brothers and sisters all over the world are going through the same kind of suffering you are (1 Peter 5:5-9, NLT).

Some of us have majored in this—we know this scripture backward and forward, and we think we know our place of authority. Just as we are to understand our place under God's authority, like I said, it's important we understand the place of authority God has in turn given us.

But your place of authority is not effective, and you cannot effectively resist the devil, until you first humble yourself under God's authority. This scripture makes it all so clear—humble yourselves so that God can exalt you.

This is authority over *as a result* of being under authority. This is the system that God created for authority.

Remember that scripture in James from earlier: "'God resists the proud, but gives grace to the humble.' Therefore submit to

God. Resist the devil and he will flee from you…. Humble your-selves in the sight of the Lord, and He will lift you up" (James 4:6-7, 10). Sometimes we quote verse 7 without considering what came directly before it or the scripture that follows it later. God resists the proud, but He lifts up the humble.

• • •

HUMBLE YOURSELVES SO THAT
GOD CAN EXALT YOU. THIS IS AUTHORITY OVER
AS A RESULT OF BEING UNDER AUTHORITY.

• • •

Notice where your place of authority over the devil comes from: It comes from your submission to God. Maybe you didn't even realize you had authority over the devil. Well, you do. You have just seen the scripture that says so. You have a name and rank that is much higher than his. So use it.

Armed With Authority

In 1 Samuel 17, we read the account of David and Goliath. Most of us know this story pretty well—David challenges the Philistine champion, Goliath, and hits him in the head with a stone from his sling. Since he has no sword, David runs up and cuts Goliath's head off with his own sword, and then the Israelites chase the Philistines into the countryside.

It's a great victory, and when the fighting is over, David is brought before King Saul—still holding Goliath's head—where he meets Saul's son, Jonathan. From that moment on, these two become best friends. In fact, the Bible tells us that their souls were knit (1 Samuel 18:1).

Because they were such fast friends, they did something today we may not understand very well—they made a covenant. First

Samuel 18:3-4 says, "Then Jonathan and David made a covenant, because he loved him as his own soul. And Jonathan took off the robe that was on him and gave it to David, with his armor, even to his sword and his bow and his belt."

This is an act that carries great significance. The things Jonathan gives David are highly symbolic, because these are all things intertwined with his identity. This wasn't just armor out of the city armory; this wasn't just any sword or any robe.

These were items that belonged to the son of the king. Those pieces of armor represented two things: name and rank.

When David had inquired what the one who beat the Philistine champion would receive, he learned that the man would receive the king's daughter in marriage. Jonathan was welcoming David as a brother, and because of their friendship, they entered into a covenant that placed Jonathan's position and responsibility on David as well. From that point on, David lived at the palace and did whatever King Saul ordered him to do.

Jonathan was saying to David, "Here, take my name. Take my rank. Take my position and authority and responsibility."

This wasn't the first offer of armor David had received. If you'll remember, before David fought Goliath, Saul offered him his own armor. Armor represents authority, and I believe when Saul recognized God's anointing on David—the anointing with which Samuel had marked David as the future king—he saw something he *used* to have.

He saw on David the anointing and presence of God that he once had himself. I believe when Saul recognized this anointing he, too, was convinced that David was about to kill this giant.

Because of that, he tried to offer David his armor so that all would see and recognize that David was fighting with Saul's approval and this victory would be won under Saul's authority. He wanted a piece of the credit for the victory, which he saw David capable of winning because of God's anointing on his life. He wanted David to go out in the name and authority of Saul, sanctioned as the king's champion.

But David didn't cooperate. He tried on Saul's armor, and he walked around in it. But it didn't fit. David told Saul he couldn't wear it because he hadn't *proven* it. He hadn't tested it.

What he had proven, what he had tested, was his faith in God, when he killed a lion and a bear to protect his sheep. He knew how to trust God and Him alone. He knew how to be under God's authority. David could not fight this fight under a man's authority; he had to fight this battle with the armor he had worn until that point—his confidence in the Most High.

So when David confronted Goliath, he didn't do it in Saul's name. Instead, he said: "You come to me with a sword, with a spear, and with a javelin. But I come to you in the name of the Lord of hosts, the God of the armies of Israel, whom you have defied" (1 Samuel 17:45).

David understood authority, and he understood God's place of authority.

•••

GOD GIVES US ARMOR—
ARMOR THAT RATIFIES HIS COVENANT.

•••

The Armor of God

Saul had armor that didn't fit David's life because it hadn't been proved; Jonathan had armor that he symbolically gave David to honor their covenant of friendship and brotherhood.

In a similar sense, God gives us armor—armor that ratifies His covenant. In Ephesians, Paul tells us about God's armor. He tells us to put it on, and he reminds us why we need it.

Finally, my brethren, be strong in the Lord and in the power of His might. Put on the whole armor of God, that you may be able to stand against the wiles of the devil. For we do not wrestle against flesh and blood, but against principalities, against powers, against the rulers of the darkness of this age, against spiritual hosts of wickedness in the heavenly places. Therefore take up the whole armor of God, that you may be able to withstand in the evil day, and having done all, to stand. Stand therefore, having girded your waist with truth, having put on the breast-plate of righteousness, and having shod your feet with the preparation of the gospel of peace; above all, taking the shield of faith with which you will be able to quench all the fiery darts of the wicked one. And take the helmet of salvation, and the sword of the Spirit, which is the word of God (Ephesians 6:10-17).

Jonathan gave David his armor as a symbol of his side of the covenant—of giving David his position as a son of the king, of his name and rank. God's armor is no different; He's giving us His armor—His Name, His rank, His authority. It represents the identity in which He wants us living and fighting the battles of life—the identity of a child of God covered in His very own authority.

•••

UNDERSTANDING GOD'S AUTHORITY
IS SO IMPORTANT BECAUSE IT GIVES US
OUR IDENTITY.

•••

Just as Jonathan gave David his armor to symbolically represent a covenant between them, giving David his own responsibility as the son of a king, so too does God give you His armor to represent the covenant He has with us, which gives us the responsibility and authority of sons and daughters of the King.

The second thing you can do to help implement an understanding of God's authority in your life is to wear this armor—put it on your life by accepting His authority and the significance behind the gift of this armor and its corresponding authority (and responsibility).

Understanding God's authority is so important because it gives us our identity. We dare not fight on our own, leaning on our own understanding. Our fight isn't with flesh and blood. But just because you can't see your enemy, don't be fooled into thinking he isn't real. You have been given the weapons of your warfare, and they are mighty *in God!* We must humble ourselves and let Him lift us up under the authority He has given us as people under His covenant and under His identity.

That position—under His authority—is what gives us authority over the principalities and powers Paul is talking about in Ephesians. It's what gives us the authority over the devil, to resist him and expect him to flee.

You never have to fight alone. You weren't born to fight alone. You weren't born to wage war on your own. God didn't create you to leave you out there with your own understanding. He didn't create you to leave you alone to rely on your own insight and your own wisdom.

How far will your own understanding get you? It will only get you as far as you've ever been. God needs people who will go further than ever before.

We Are His Name

This name and this rank that we've been talking about is amazing, because in and of ourselves, we're nowhere near it. We are nothing, know nothing, have nothing, and can do nothing on our own. But when we humble ourselves, obey the leading of the Spirit of God, take our place in Christ Jesus, and recognize the source of our authority, we take our place of authority. When we do these things, we represent His nature to those around us.

You and I are His name on the earth.

What is the quickest way to see mercy in your life? Be merciful. Look for God's mercy in operation in your life. You're looking for the authority of God. You're looking for God to take His place in your life, and the quickest way to do it is by being humble and accepting His authority. Humble yourself under the mighty hand of God that He may exalt you. Accept His armor, which represents His name and rank, and thus His authority. Then take your place. Exercise your authority.

• • •

WE MAY SPEAK TO OUR
CIRCUMSTANCES WITH THE AUTHORITY
AND POWER OF JESUS' NAME.

• • •

When we look for these character traits and these attributes of God, the quickest way for our eyes to be open to them is to see them first in ourselves. Because they're in there. You are born again; re-created life is inside of you. The authority of God Himself, the Most High, is in you, and it's on you, and it will carry you all throughout your life.

It is my prayer that as we get to know God and His personality better, He will find us submitting to His authority over us, and us exercising our own authority over the forces of darkness.

Out of this humility comes a greater confidence in Him—the same type of faith that the Roman centurion had in Jesus when he asked Him to heal his servant. Out of this confidence comes a realization that He that is in us is greater than he that is in the world (1 John 4:4).

This humility can birth an understanding of our true identity—identity derived from the covenant God has made with us, forged in Jesus' blood. It is this identity that gives us the authority in which He wants us to walk.

In the midst of a paradoxical moment of total humility and absolute boldness, we can take on the armor of God, which symbolizes His name and His rank—His authority.

As a result of this authority, we may speak to our circumstances with the authority and power of Jesus' Name—the highest Name that is named. Why? Because the whole family in heaven and on earth has been named after Him!

Condemnation has to bow its knee to the Name of Jesus—I Am is our mercy. I Am is our forgiveness. "Yes, Lord, but I don't feel forgiven." *Feeling* forgiven has nothing to do with *being* forgiven. You are forgiven *because He said so.*

Sickness has to bow its knee to the Name of Jesus—I Am says He is our healer. You are healed *because He said so.*

Depression must bow its knee to the Name of Jesus—I Am says He is our joy. Lack must bow before Jesus—I Am says He is our provider.

Isolation must bend down low before Him—I Am says that He is our Father, that Jesus calls us brother, and that the Holy Spirit is with us always.

I encourage you to take a moment to humble yourself under the mighty hand of God. Just allow Him to reveal to you any place where pride has crept in. Allow Him to reveal to you any place where you have thought that something was because of how good *you* were. Let Him reveal to you His goodness and mercy.

Let Him reveal to you anywhere in your life where you've been leaning on your own understanding, your own authority. Let Him reveal to you His authority.

When we do this—when we see His goodness and authority—He can take whatever is good in your life and make it grow and become bigger and better because of the goodness, mercy, and authority of God poured out on you.

But it takes learning about Him—it requires learning to listen for His still, small voice in your life so that He does not have to show up with a name tag on before you'll recognize Him. It takes times of reflection, of asking Him to expose anywhere in your life where you're prideful and leaning on your own understanding.

Humble yourself to the authority of God. Then rise and take your God-given place seated next to Him as His son or daughter. Through Jesus we have been adopted into the family of Father God. Let's take a look at how important it is to accept His mercy under His authority as our Father.

SECTION IV

OUR FATHER

Chapter Ten

ONLY BELIEVE

We have already looked at a few aspects of God's character as we begin to get to know Him better. We've explored God's mercy—His enduring, unearned favor and grace toward us— which changed all the rules. We've looked at how misunderstood this aspect of God can be but how the Bible proves out that God, who is the same yesterday, today, and forever, is a good and merciful God. All good things come from Him—*all* of them— and we must remember that.

It's important to remember every good thing in our lives is a result of His mercy, because thoughts like this will keep us out of pride. And as we learned in the previous section on recognizing God's authority, pride is a roadblock to understanding God's authority.

It's hard to be under His authority when you don't recognize His right to be over you—and thus be merciful to you. But when you don't accept His position of authority as Most High, you can't step into the position as a son or daughter of God that He intends for you to occupy. Remember, everything we study as an attribute of God's character is rooted in His outlandish love for us. He loves because He is love.

•••

REMEMBER—EVERY GOOD THING IN OUR LIVES IS A RESULT OF HIS MERCY.

•••

I want to show you another aspect of God that some have an easier time understanding than others—that of God as our Father. Most children in some way want to grow up and be like their parents; at some point, most little boys imitate their fathers and want to be just like them. Little girls are usually the same way. Some of us have harsh circumstances that kill that desire within us, but typically, little children don't know any better than to love and emulate their parents.

I had a good upbringing and am happy to be growing up much like my father—even though there are those moments I find my-self doing some of the same things my family has teased my dad about for years. But my dad, George Pearsons, is a good man, and if I am going to be teased for being like someone, I am glad it is him.

You really don't have to be a psychologist to study a pattern of children growing up to be like their parents. I look back across my life, and I am fascinated to see things that began in my father's father now living in me.

My grandfather Horace C. Pearsons was one of my favorite people ever. He and my grandmother lived on Cape Cod in Massachusetts, and I grew up in Fort Worth, Texas, so I only got to see them once or twice a year.

I think I was so taken with him because of his amazing artistic abilities. I would watch him draw and wanted so badly to be able to do what I saw him do. He spent his career as a graphic designer, working some in advertising in New York City, then later as the head of his own design company. He was mostly retired by the time I came along, which meant there was plenty of time for me to say, "Draw me a picture, Grandpa!" and he would.

He would sit in his big chair in the living room with a small white pad of paper and his black felt-tip pen and then come up with some of the most outrageous cartoons and characters I had ever seen. He drew literally hundreds and hundreds of pictures for me, and to this day I love to sit and go through them.

Why? Because each one reminds me of Grandpa. They all have a little bit of him in them.

Of course, my dad was no stranger to this while he was growing up. He, too, would sit and watch his father work and draw and design. By the time my dad was in early high school, he had already decided he was going to spend his life in art and music. As a result of this decision, he was convinced he had no need for math and science and that high school was now just something standing between him and art school. His dream was to attend art school in Boston, graduate, then ride the New York City subway every day to work in advertising. Just like his father.

He did graduate from high school and go to art school in Boston. But in 1972, on break from school, my dad asked Jesus to be the Lord of his life while standing at the top of the stairs in my grandparents' house—the same house I visited all those years when I would sit and watch Grandpa draw.

Though that decision radically altered the course of my dad's life, the desire to create and design never left him. He moved from Cape Cod, Massachusetts, to Tulsa, Oklahoma, which was like traveling internationally or even to another planet.

While attending Oral Roberts University, he met Terri Copeland, my mom, fell in love, and got engaged. Terri's father, Kenneth—a relatively unknown preacher at that time—was less than ten years into full-time ministry.

In the summer of 1976, my dad moved to Fort Worth, Texas,

at the invitation of his fiancée's father, and became the graphic designer for Kenneth Copeland Evangelistic Association. He has now been with Kenneth Copeland Ministries for over thirty years. He calls it the longest summer job he's ever had.

For many of those years he was responsible for all of the print publications for the ministry. He watched their newsletter grow from a two-color, four-page print job, to a full-color, thirty-two-page magazine that is sent free of charge every month to over 400,000 people in homes and churches around the world.

At the time I am writing this, he has been pastor of our church for the past sixteen years.

And though that is a far cry from traveling via subway in New York City every day, I still see those same gifts, talents, and abilities at work in my dad that were first in his father. My dad's creativity and artistic side shine through often while he is in the pulpit preaching and relating to people.

While many fathers and sons would spend summer evenings in the driveway working on how to throw a curve ball, my dad and I spent our time at the piano playing Beatles' songs and trying to come up with really cool chords.

That love for art, music, and all things creative that first existed in my grandfather Horace is still alive in me today, and I got it from watching my dad. I even played the exact same saxophone in high school that he did.

Dad and I tease each other about the days we didn't spend hunting, fishing, and camping. But the quality time we did spend together is a major contribution to who I am today.

On a side note, I did play sports growing up. But it was mom with me in the driveway teaching me to catch and throw. Dad was there, but with the video camera surgically attached to his shoulder so he'd have footage for the short film he created at the end of every baseball season.

I see so much of my father in me. And others do too. And it's not just his creative side I inherited. It is his compassion for people and desire to give to others that I find swelling up in me almost uncontrollably at times. It may sound like I am bragging on myself, but really I am bragging on him and the nature of God I see inside him. I have often said that one of the greatest compliments I've ever had was when someone said, "Jeremy, you're so much like your father."

To anyone who has said or thought that, I say, "Thank you."

I realize this is not everyone's story. I realize many have had harsh experiences with their earthly fathers, but I only tell you these things to illustrate a point that can prove to be true in anyone's life:

We become who—or what—we spend our time with.

• • •

ABRAHAM BELIEVED GOD,
AND GOD COUNTED HIM RIGHTEOUS
BECAUSE OF HIS FAITH.

• • •

The Abraham Connection

I want to show you something that is both simple and profound. I love simple things—things I can apply, things I can actually do. I like practical things, and I believe that this section on recognizing that character of God as our Father will be like that for us—simple but profound and easy to apply.

I want to talk about a man commonly referred to as Father Abraham. Although his life dates back to the Old Testament and is recorded in the book of Genesis, we are going to look first of all in the New Testament.

Romans 4 tells us about Abraham, beginning with the first two verses. I encourage you to read this whole chapter, but we're going to draw out the salient points. Verses 1-2 say, "What then shall we say that Abraham our father has found according to the flesh? For if Abraham was justified by works, he has something to boast about, but not before God."

In many ways, if anyone could boast it would be Abraham. If he were justified by what he did outwardly or by being obedient to some law, Abraham would have had something to boast about, because he really did a lot.

But it isn't about works. We read on as it says Abraham believed God and that God counted him righteous because of his faith. It wasn't something he earned through work; it was a gift he received because of his faith.

"Abraham believed God" (verse 3). This is a very important statement. What have I told you Jesus is looking for in us, and from us, just as with the Samaritan woman at the well we read about at the beginning of the book?

Belief.

Abraham believed God, and God accounted it to him as righteousness. God was looking for it then, Jesus looked for it while He was on the earth, and God seeks it from us today. Belief.

Paul tells us that the symbol God gave Abraham to mark him as God's, to show that he believed, was circumcision—a cutting away of the flesh. Although I find it awkward to talk and write about, I don't think enough is made out of the significance of circumcision, of how much trust Abraham needed to have in God to carry out this act of obedience. But it was a symbol that Abraham already had faith and that God had already accepted him and declared him to be righteous—even before he was circumcised.

This faith Abraham had was very special, because it made him the spiritual father of all of us who have faith. Accepting Jesus is a spiritual circumcision, as putting our flesh up on the cross with Christ is definitely a cutting away of something sensitive. So just as Abraham was counted righteous not because of what he did, but because of in whom he *believed,* we too are counted righteous because of our faith.

Verse 11 tells us Abraham was the "father of all those who believe." Not just Jews, but you and me—Christians. The same merciful God who called Abraham out of the land of his fathers and to a place of promise, to father His holy nation, has extended His mercy to us through Jesus Christ.

If God called Paul to preach one thing, if there is one component you can trace throughout his writings in the New Testament, you will find it is this: Paul teaches that it is not about the Law; it is not about works. Paul preaches about renewing your mind to grace—renewing your mind to salvation by faith through grace.

And when we read about Abraham in Romans, Paul is in the middle of comparing works to grace, works to believing, and works to faith.

I want you to ask yourself a question that I have asked before; let's see if we come up with the same answer. Why would the Spirit of God inspire Paul to backtrack so far in the past to highlight a man, Abraham, who lived under the old covenant when he was teaching about a "new and better" covenant? Why did God go that far in reverse to preach the message of Jesus Christ?

I believe the answer to our question can be found in verse 13, "Clearly, God's promise to give the whole earth to Abraham and his descendants was based not on his obedience to God's law, but on a right relationship with God that comes by faith" (NLT). God never intended to make the promise dependent on keeping the law; it's *always* been about righteousness through faith. Paul was taking people back to a time before the Law of Moses.

Hello, Abraham. My Name Is God.

I want to look at one particular statement that God said to Abraham in Genesis 12. God introduced Himself to this man. He said, "Hello. My name is God. And this is what I'm going to do for you. I am going to make you the father of many nations. Look up at the stars. As many as you can number, that will be your descendants; the sand on the shore, that is the nation that is coming out of you. You will be the heir of the world. And the people that bless you, I will bless. The ones that curse you, I will curse." (See also Genesis 22:17 and Romans 4:13.)

God's mercy and favor were all over Abraham. He even entered covenant with this man He had called out from among his father's people. Abraham accepted, and God's authority covered him.

•••

ABRAHAM'S WAS NOT A COVENANT OF RULES; GOD COUNTED ABRAHAM RIGHTEOUS BECAUSE HE BELIEVED.

•••

But this was not a covenant of rules; God counted Abraham righteous because he *believed.* And notice that what Abraham believed was not based on what Abraham could see. As a matter of fact, there was a serious lack of evidence and an even greater absence of logic to back up what God was saying to him. But there was a voice that rose up louder than doubt.

It was the voice of faith. Abraham had *faith.* It wasn't about what he could or could not see, it was about what he would or would not believe.

Paul used the life of Abraham to preach the message of Jesus because faith existed before the Law. Long before God gave the

•••

IT WASN'T ABOUT WHAT HE COULD OR COULD NOT SEE, IT WAS ABOUT WHAT HE WOULD OR WOULD NOT BELIEVE.

•••

Law to Moses, He made a covenant with Abraham because he believed and God counted it to him as righteousness.

It was only generations later, after this one man had founded a nation millions strong, that God delivered them from Egypt and gave them rules to follow. He gave them the top ten, and then the next hundreds that followed, because this people needed to be taught how to live. They were saturated in another—pagan— culture, and He had to show them the way to live.

•••

YOU'VE GOT TO UNLEARN THE
MISTAKEN THOUGHT THAT GOD IS ONLY
INTERESTED IN RULES AND REGULLATIONS.

•••

But one thing came before any of that—before the Ten Commandments, before all the rules and regulations. *Faith.* They had to believe that God existed. Belief preceded the Law.

Remember I said I like to keep it simple? So does God. He made it simple from the beginning: Believe in God. In His conversation with the woman at the well, Jesus looked at her and said, "Believe Me, woman..."

The need for belief existed before the Law ever showed up, before the rules ever came on the scene. And that is why Paul, writing to the Romans, had to help them unlearn some of the misdirected foundation of the Jewish religion as he illuminated their thinking on the difference between the Law and grace.

You've got to unlearn the mistaken thought that God is only interested in rules and regulations—that He is nothing more than a divine rule-maker. You've got to unlearn the idea that you can be righteous by keeping all the rules. You've got to unlearn trying to do what's right, even though you can't seem to find the strength. You've got to unlearn guilt, unlearn shame, unlearn condemnation, and you must be introduced to this concept called grace.

Paul looked back at a man before the Law, at a man who simply believed in God and would pass that belief on to his children. That is why God used the illustration of this man to help unlearn religion, to help unlearn tradition. He had to help us unlearn what it became—God the rule-maker—for what it should have been.

We've got to learn that, like Abraham, God is a Father to His people. So what was so special about Abraham and the way he believed that God chose to make him the father of all who believe? Read on and we'll find out.

Chapter Eleven

WHAT DID YOU SAY YOUR NAME WAS?

God saw Abraham as righteous because he believed. Abraham lived by faith before there even was a Law. Faith was his Law. Faith was his rule.

And what did God make him? A father. The father of all who believe. Paul goes on to say, "As it is written: 'I have made you a father of many nations.' He is our father in the sight of God, in whom he believed—the God who gives life to the dead and calls things that are not as though they were" (Romans 4:17, NIV).

•••

ABRAHAM LIVED BY FAITH
BEFORE THERE EVEN WAS A LAW.
FAITH WAS HIS LAW.

•••

This sounds like Faith 101 here. Everything we know about faith, it all came from the example of Father Abraham. The Word tells us why:

> Against all hope, Abraham in hope believed and so became the father of many nations, just as it had been said to him, "So shall your offspring be." Without weakening in his faith, he faced the fact that his body was as good as dead—since he was about a hundred years old—and that Sarah's womb was also dead. Yet he did not waver through unbelief regarding the promise of God, but was strengthened in his faith and gave glory to God, being fully persuaded that God had power to do what he had promised. This is why "it was credited to him as righteousness" (verses 18-22, NIV).

You want to know why this man had found such favor in the sight of God? Why this man was called righteous when no other man on earth was given that title? Because of the way he believed.

He was fully convinced, fully persuaded, that God could do what He said He would; he did not waver at the promise of God and did not consider his own body to be dead or the deadness of Sarah's womb. No other factor had anything to do with it.

And this is the example Abraham set for his children. This is why the apostle Paul could say, "Live like this. Get your mind off the rules. Get your mind off of trying harder. Get your head over into faith. This thing—this new life that has been planted inside of you—let that seed spring up and produce something in you. Stop considering everything else around you. Live like this man, our spiritual father, Abraham."

Father of Those Who Believe

Abraham believed, and God counted it to him as righteousness. Now we consider ourselves to be believers. My concern, however, is that the term "believer" may be being applied a little more loosely than how Paul used it in reference to Abraham and the character of his life.

What is a "believer"? Who is a "believer"? Are you a "believer"? A "believer" in what? It's a title we've given ourselves, and I believe to an extent that it's probably very fitting. This is a word that we use to define our lives—define the way we live, define our attitude toward God. But in comparison, do we believe the same way that Abraham did?

The Spirit of God inspired Paul to use this man as an example of having faith and to help us understand the message of the gospel. He preached Jesus by preaching Abraham.

So I wanted to find out how he believed, and we're going to find out what faith looks like.

In Genesis 15, we read the account of God's covenant with Abraham, then named Abram. It seems that God is big on changing people's names. It happens a couple of times in the first book of the Bible alone. After Abram had followed the Lord's leading to depart from the land of his fathers, God spoke to him again and promised to protect and reward him.

But Abram had a major problem: He had no children. The "father of many nations" should have at least one child—preferably a son. And so he tells God that all His blessings are wonderful, but they mean little without a son. Abram had no heir, so all of God's blessings would either die with him or pass on to one of his servants.

So God promises him that his servant won't be his heir and that He is going to give him a son. God takes him outside and shows him the sky. "'Look now toward heaven, and count the stars if you are able to number them.' And He said to him, 'So shall your descendants be'" (verse 5).

And here it is—the key verse. Having heard God's promise,

understanding all of the problems we discussed earlier, such as his age and Sarah's, it says this: "And Abram believed the Lord, and the Lord counted him as righteous because of his faith" (verse 6, NLT).

•••

GOD SAID IT, ABRAHAM BELIEVED IT. PERIOD.

•••

God said it, he believed it. Period. Remember we talked about *because I said so?* He lived in this mentality with God, giving God His rightful place of authority in his life. God said it—and that was enough for Abram.

He believed.

It's hard for us to put ourselves in his shoes because we have the benefit of reading the rest of the story. We know about Isaac, the child of promise, and all that came after. But try not to think about that. Try to put yourself before any of this had been fulfilled, truly in Abraham's perspective when there was no proof.

This is a man named Abram who has no child, who has no proof, but who believes that God is at work in his life. He has only God's word on it. There's nothing outwardly to prove what's going on. He's experiencing favor in some areas. He's won some battles. But when it comes down to him being the father of many nations, there's nothing to prove it so far.

Nothing. And yet he says, "I believe."

And what happens next? Not a whole lot—no proof. In fact, in his advancing age Abram takes his wife's servant into his tent and conceives Ishmael. And that is no good—Ishmael wasn't the promise. This wasn't the way God promised to do it.

And *thirteen years* follow where *nothing* happens.

But in Romans, Paul tells us Abram's faith did not weaken or waver—despite closing in on 100 years old, still he kept hoping!

He was fully convinced that God was able to do whatever He promised. In fact, Paul tells us that Abram's faith grew *stronger*.

And this takes us to Genesis 17, where God comes to Abram again and says,

> "I am Almighty God; walk before Me and be blameless. And I will make My covenant between Me and you, and will multiply you exceedingly." Then Abram fell on his face, and God talked with him, saying: "As for Me, behold, My covenant is with you, and you shall be a father of many nations. No longer shall your name be called Abram, but your name shall be Abraham; for I have made you a father of many nations" (verses 1-5).

God shows up and establishes a covenant between them. When God changes his name from Abram to Abraham, He changes his entire identity. God changes him from a childless man to the father of many nations and the father of faith.

•••

ABRAHAM KNEW GOD
WELL ENOUGH TO TRUST HIM—
TO HAVE FAITH IN HIS WORD TO HIM.

•••

Believing as Abraham Did

What does it really mean to believe, as Abraham believed? It all comes back to faith. Abraham believed God could and would do what He said He would do. He knew God well enough to trust Him—to have faith in His word to him.

And sure enough, God shows up. Once again He introduces

Himself to Abraham in a big way and then says, "I am changing your name."

Now let's think about this for a second. This name, Abram, has worked well for the last ninety-nine years or so, but God shows up and says, "I am changing your name."

Why?

Well, this is why we had to cover both mercy and authority first—God was already having mercy on Abram, blessing and prospering him. But what did we say about authority? It's about name and rank.

So God was saying, "I am changing your identity. I am changing your authority. No longer is your name Abram. Your name is now Abraham. You are connected to Me."

It's easy for us to read about Abram getting his name changed, but just think about it for a moment—he's had this name for *ninety-nine years!* How would we feel if God changed *our* names? What if God were to show up tomorrow morning bright and early in our room, introduce Himself in a big way, and say, "We need to change your name"?

One of the first things on our mind would be, "What are people going to think about this?" We'd probably think about having to get our driver's license changed and how we'll have to get new return address stickers for our mail. And all that would come after we had gotten over the initial shock of seeing God. That is, of course, assuming we recognized Him in the first place.

I might try to bargain with Him: "Lord, I'll tell You what… That's good—I like it. It's strong. What You and I are going to do, we're going to keep that between us; and while "Jeremyham" does have a certain ring to it, if I tell other people, they will think I'm crazy. And I don't want to mess up my testimony with them. So, me and You—You change my name, and when You call me I'll answer. No one else needs to know."

But that's not the way—that's not the example that Abraham set. That's not *believing.* It's not trusting God.

God spoke, and Abraham said, "OK." *Because I said so.* Abraham was able to do this because he recognized God's mercy and because of the place of authority he gave God.

He took God's *word* to him and changed his *world* to fit that word. All too often we're tempted to take His Word and try to change it to fit our world. But that's not faith, and I don't think that it pleases Him.

You can't rely on your own understanding when you believe God and step out in faith, as Abraham did. Your own experience can only take you as far as you have been, but faith will get you out into God's will—into the unfamiliar, into new places, where you have no choice but to rely on Him.

Abraham heard from the Lord, and he took God's word to him and made his thinking fit what God said. No questions asked.

Cutting Away the Flesh

Changing Abraham's name isn't all God did. Later in Genesis 17, God instructs Abraham concerning circumcision. God wanted Abraham circumcised and that he do the same for every male child born in his family line. In fact, *every* male in his household, servants included, was to be circumcised. God told Abraham that circumcision "shall be a sign of the covenant between Me and you" (verse 11).

Now, you must understand that Abraham had a *big* household. He was like a king, with all manner of servants and other members of his extended household. And *all* the men had to have this done. That's a pretty big job.

And here's something else that's interesting about Abraham. A few verses down, we read that Abraham got around to obeying God and performing this extensive, pretty delicate task "that very same day" (verse 23). Remember what we talked about regarding "God working on you" about something—

taking a long time to obey? Well, that's not faith, either; that's not belief as Abraham believed.

I think it probably went something like this: I'm thinking Abraham probably called everybody together for a big "company" meeting. Sarah (whose name used to be Sarai, incidentally; God was really in the name-changing mood that day), Ishmael, Hagar—everybody. All the servants, all the foreigners, everyone who was born in the house.

So who knows how many people are standing there, and you've got guys kind of staying in the back; you know, they just work for the man. They don't really know him. They're just standing there, wondering, "What does he want to talk about today?" "I don't know. Just called a meeting."

So Abraham says, "I'd like to call this meeting to order, and I've got a few things here on the agenda. First of all, I want to let you know that some of you guys over here need to take better care of the sheep. They're kind of getting out over there. And if we can get some of the cattle roped in over here.

"Also," he went on, "I, ah, I'm changing my name—just so you know."

Everybody says, "Changing your name? But sir, you're so...old. Why now? You know, a midlife crisis was a long time ago. What's going on?"

And he says, "That's right, I'm changing my name. You know me as Abram. But I talked with God today. He came down this morning. He just left like fifteen minutes ago. We spent some time together, and He is changing my name. Now you must call me Abraham."

And maybe as an afterthought, he looks around for his wife and says, "Sarai? Yeah, I also want to let you know—sweetie, God's changing your name too. You're now Sarah."

Now for the bombshell: "Ah, OK, guys...there's one other thing God talked to me about. I'm not too familiar with this, but the circumcisions will begin right after the meeting. All the men—everyone older than eight days—let's just go ahead and form a single-file line behind my tent, OK?"

• • •

ABRAHAM DID NOT DELAY
IN SHOWING THAT HE BELIEVED;
HE ACTED. IMMEDIATELY.

• • •

I'm sure this went over really well with the servants. There was probably one guy in the back with a cold wishing he'd called in sick that day. But Abraham wasn't messing around. God told him that day, and he did it *that day.* And what about Ishmael? If I'm a 13-year-old kid and I hear this is going on, I'm thinking to myself, *I can run faster than you, old man.*

In the face of certain opposition, Abraham had the boldness to stand up and say, "I have heard from God. He said to do this, and we're doing it." He had met with God, and Abraham did not delay in showing that he believed; he acted. Immediately. Because God said so.

He did it the same day—maybe the same hour. I wouldn't have faulted him for thinking about it for a while or asking God for more time. But you know what? Not Abraham. "Change my name. Change my wife's name. Now we're going to put a mark on our flesh that says we believe in the Name of the Lord. This is who we are. This is what we do. This is our lives. This is what we believe. This is how we live. This is what we base the whole thing on. Proof that we believe."

This 99-year-old man changed his entire world to fit the word that God spoke to him. It didn't matter what had to change or how much it hurt to do it. You'd think that Abraham, like most of us, would be slow to change his ways. But he changed it all in a moment when the Lord spoke.

This is what it means to believe.

Proof of Faith

There is one other thing that I find particularly remarkable about Abraham. After Isaac, the son of promise, is indeed born to Abraham and Sarah, fulfilling God's promise of an heir to him, there is one final hurdle that Abraham's belief must cross.

In Genesis 22 we pick up the narrative some years after Isaac's birth when God again speaks to Abraham. But this time, it seems incongruous.

> Now it came to pass after these things that God tested Abraham, and said to him, "Abraham!" And he said, "Here I am." Then He said, "Take now your son, your only son Isaac, whom you love, and go to the land of Moriah, and offer him there as a burnt offering on one of the mountains of which I shall tell you" (verses 1-2).

Imagine the disconnect! This boy, the son of promise God had provided, is to die as a sacrifice. But true to form, Abraham doesn't ask "why" or delay; early the next morning, he saddles his donkey and takes off with Isaac and a couple of servants.

When they get to the place God indicated, Abraham has the servants stay behind, and only he and Isaac go forward to worship. Isaac, in fact, carries the wood for the offering—the sacrifice at which he's the guest of honor.

Now, Isaac must have been reasonably old by this point—old enough to carry the wood, and he's a sharp one. He notices something wasn't quite right. "Isaac turned to Abraham and said, 'Father?' 'Yes, my son?' Abraham replied. 'We have the fire and the wood,' the boy said, 'but where is the sheep for the burnt offering?'" (verse 7, NLT).

Now listen to Abraham's reply, firm in his belief and obedience: "My son, God will provide for Himself the lamb for a burnt of-fering" (verse 8).

That apparently was enough, and the two of them went on together to the place God had told Abraham about. He proceeds to build an altar with the wood…and then to *bind Isaac on it.*

God takes it right to the very edge. Abraham is literally pulling out the knife, drawing it from its sheath and is looking God's promise—his only son—in the face as he's ready to slay him for the sacrifice. Think about that! He's about to kill his son *because God said so!*

But right then, right at the last possible moment, God intervenes:

> But the Angel of the Lord called to him from heaven and said, "Abraham, Abraham!" So he said, "Here I am." And He said, "Do not lay your hand on the lad, or do anything to him; for now I know that you fear God, since you have not withheld your son, your only son, from Me" (verses 11-12).

God took it right to the wire, and Abraham held fast. He stood firm in his belief, and when he was right there at the brink, God called out to him and provided a ram for an offering.

In the epic faith chapter of Hebrews, the writer sums this up so perfectly:

> It was by faith that Abraham offered Isaac as a sacrifice when God was testing him. Abraham, who had received God's promises, was ready to sacrifice his only son, Isaac, even though God had told him, "Isaac is the son through whom your descendants will be counted." Abraham reasoned that if Isaac died, God was able to bring him back to life again. And in a sense, Abraham did receive his son back from the dead (Hebrews 11:17-19, NLT).

Not only did this man change his name—not only did this man endure and endure year after year while waiting on the Lord to make good on His promise, but this man had shed his own blood by putting a mark on his own flesh that proved that he believed. Now this man was willing to sacrifice that very promise *because God said so.*

God asked him to sacrifice his blessing on the altar before Him, and without a moment's hesitation, Abraham obeyed.

This is what it means to believe regardless of what God tells you. This is immediate, unswerving obedience. And it is this very belief that so set apart Abraham and qualified him to be the father of all who believe.

•••

GOD ASKED HIM TO SACRIFICE HIS BLESSING, AND WITHOUT A MOMENT'S HESITATION, ABRAHAM OBEYED.

•••

Like Abraham, we must shape our worlds to fit the Word of God. Whatever has to change must change—that is what it means to believe.

I trust it's becoming increasingly clear why Paul used Abraham as his example in Romans. Abraham took belief far beyond the level most of us understand. The father of those who believe set the bar pretty high.

But yet recall what I said at the beginning of the section: Abraham did a lot—he could really brag about how long he hoped, how God changed his name, how he was willing to put his flesh in agony, and how he was willing to sacrifice his son—but none of this is what mattered to God. If you stack all of those things up and put them before God, they're nothing.

Paul says it wasn't his works, it was the fact that he believed. Belief produced the works. Abraham did what he did because of what he believed.

But Abraham is not just a father of those who believe because he himself believed; perhaps more importantly, he taught his son Isaac to believe as well...

Chapter Twelve

HAVE YOU SEEN MY FATHER?

I've endured some days in my life that tested my belief. There was one in particular that I was not looking forward to and knew was going to be one of the hardest days of my life. Because of the situation and circumstances, I had to do it on my own and my father couldn't be there—it wasn't a day for having family around.

So instead he gave me something to take with me—a stack of photocopied scriptures he had highlighted—to keep my eyes on instead of my circumstances. They were scriptures about deliverance and about God's faithfulness. He sat down with me, and we walked through them together before I walked into the lion's den. He said, "You keep your eyes on this. You hold on to this."

And all throughout that day, I didn't take my eyes off those scriptures.

While I was sitting there in the middle of one of the worst days of my life, do you think I was busy wishing my dad had taught me to play catch? Do you think I was lamenting that we hadn't hunted together more? I wasn't even thinking about the times around the piano or being artistic.

No. I was so grateful my father had taught me to believe. He taught me what to put faith in. He taught me what to hold on to. None of that other stuff—as good as it is—is eternal, and it will not save my life. My father taught me something of eternal value: believing in the Lord.

In the previous sections, I have given you two things that I think will help you get to know God better and that will help you listen for and hear His still, small voice, rather than forcing Him to overwhelm you before you notice Him.

In this section, we're talking about Abraham's example as the father of those who believe, and what our own Father God desires of us. God desires the same thing of you and me as Jesus did of the woman at the well—belief.

So the first thing that I believe will help you come to a more intimate, understanding relationship with God is simply this: Learn to believe. Abraham believed God, and God counted it as righteousness. That was the plan long before there was a Law to keep. He was the father of all of us who believe, those who pursue Jesus, and I suggest that we learn to walk in this spiritual father's footsteps by learning to believe God without question and to obey without preamble.

...

"You WANT TO SEE THE FATHER?
LOOK AT ME."

...

See Jesus, See the Father

I'd like to look at one more scripture to illustrate this to you. Jesus is speaking: "I am the way, the truth, and the life. No one comes to the Father except through me. If you had known Me, you would have known My Father also; and from now on you know Him and have seen Him" (John 14:6-7).

And Philip—like the woman at the well and like a lot of us who are not always quick to pick up on what God is saying—tells Jesus, "Lord, show us the Father, and it is sufficient for us" (verse 8). Jesus looks at him and says, "Have I been with you so long, and yet you have not known Me, Philip? He who has seen Me has seen the Father" (verse 9).

In other words, He looks at Philip and says, "Hello. My name is God. You want to see the Father?" He says, "Look at Me."

Jesus was the Son, and He was just like His Father. He'd wanted to be more like His Father since He was a boy, when His parents lost Him in Jerusalem and later found Him in the Temple. He was about His Father's business from the beginning.

So in being with Jesus, they had seen the Father. And Jesus didn't do anything unless He'd seen the Father do it.

Jesus starts talking to them about believing, saying,

> Do you not believe that I am in the Father, and the Father in Me? The words that I speak to you I do not speak on My own authority; but the Father who dwells in Me does the works. Believe Me that I am in the Father and the Father in Me... (verses 10-11).

And if they couldn't believe that, Jesus appealed to what they could see: "Or else believe Me for the sake of the works themselves. Most assuredly, I say to you, he who believes in Me, the works that I do he will do also; and greater works than these he will do."

Why? "Because I go to My Father. And whatever you ask in My name, that I will do, that the Father may be glorified in the Son. If you ask anything in My name, I will do it" (verses 12-14).

He Shows Us the Father

I started seriously thinking about that scripture one day, just thinking about believing, and I started going through it piece by piece.

"He who believes in Me," Jesus says. Well, I believe in Him. I believe He is the Son of God. I believe He came to this earth. I believe He lived a sinless, spotless life. I believe He healed people—opened blind eyes and deaf ears, made lame legs to walk, and raised people from the dead. I believe it. I'm going to shape my life around it.

What am I doing by thinking along those lines? I am filling the blank. God is _____. I am answering Jesus' question to His disciples, "Who do you say that I am?"

He says, "If you believe in Me, (which I do) then the works that I do you will do also." Jesus is in the Father, He says, and we are in Him—so we are in the Father and we see the Father through Him! When we look at Jesus, we see the Father. And Jesus tells us we can do those same things He did—in His name and under His authority. We can see ourselves doing the same things Jesus did.

Jesus laid hands on people and they recovered; Jesus was compassionate and merciful to people; Jesus preached the gospel to the poor, brought sight to the blind, liberty to the captives and healing to the brokenhearted. We too can do these things!

That might challenge someone's traditional, religious way of thinking, but I didn't say it. He did! And how are we able to do the things He did? Because we've earned the right to more power through our good deeds and impeccable record of law-keeping? No! It's because we are believers.

And then Jesus makes this very important statement: "And greater works than these you will do." When I read that—really *read* it—I nearly choked. *Greater?* Now, I can believe in Him, and I can believe that through Him we can do the same things He did because He told us it is so. But greater things than Jesus Christ did? What can this possibly mean for our lives?

To me, it means we haven't seen anything yet! And it means we can't be dependent on our experience or lack thereof. We are solely dependent on and qualified by what and in whom we believe!

Belief Can Shape Your World

Abraham-like belief takes this statement and shapes its world to fit what the Word of God says. And that is the second practical step I give you: Don't stop with belief, but use your belief to shape your world to fit what God has told you. If God says it in His Word, treat it as true no matter what the evidence says to the contrary. If God gives you a promise, stand on it, no matter how long it takes.

Let God's truth shape your world.

Mere "good" works did not mark Abraham's life. They were "great" works. Think about it. He changed his name, he shed his blood, and he was willing to sacrifice his only son. But it wasn't the works that impressed God. It was the belief that gave birth to those works.

•••

ABRAHAM-LIKE BELIEF SHAPES ITS WORLD TO FIT WHAT THE WORD OF GOD SAYS.

•••

Pastor Joseph Prince, one who many consider an expert in the arena of the grace of God, has said many times before, "Right believing leads to right living."

Now that we have a clear picture of what it means to believe, I want you to hold your life as a believer up against what you've seen from the life of Abraham. Are you as determined to follow the leading of God at that great a cost? How quickly do you jump to your feet in obedience when you receive direction or correction?

But let me make something clear. I am not telling you that to qualify as a believer you have to go right out and change your name, shed your blood, or offer your firstborn child on the altar.

Why are we exempt from those acts? Because we are believers! We *believe* that when we made Jesus the Lord of our lives He gave us a new name—His name! Your name has already been changed! Do you *believe* it?

And with that new name came a new identity. You are a new creation in Christ Jesus. *Believe* it!

We don't shed our own blood because we *believe* in the blood that Jesus shed for us on the cross. We are not required to sacrifice our sons because we *believe* in the only begotten Son of God who was sacrificed for us.

Now, let that way of believing produce right living in you. Live as though your name has been changed, as though you were purchased back by the blood of Jesus, and as though God paid the highest price imaginable just for you. Let that way of believing set your boundaries for right living.

Live what you believe.

Be Like Your Father

When I preach this message, I again hand out name tags. When teaching on mercy, we fill out and wear a name tag bearing "Mercy." When teaching on God's authority, we fill out name tags bearing, "Humility."

Jesus said that if they had seen the Son, they had seen the Father. The highest goal to which we can aspire is being like our Father. Like I mentioned earlier in this chapter, the greatest compliment I have ever received wasn't about a message I preached or a song I played; it was, "Jeremy, you remind me so much of your dad."

I have had a good father to look up to and emulate. He truly taught me to believe. Because if I can be a man of compassion as I've seen him be a man of compassion, if I can be a man of mercy the way I've seen him be a man of mercy, if I can treat a woman the way I've seen him treat my mother, if I can be a man of honor the way I've watched him honor the rest of my family, if I can be a man of sacrifice the way I've seen him lay down his life for people around him and for his congregation, if I can be a man of the Word, even a little bit like he is, I believe that I would bless the world.

I'd like to say, "If you have seen me, you have seen my father."

•••

HE WAS TEACHING ME TO BELIEVE
THAT IT TRULY TAKES ONLY
A FEW MINUTES OF REACHING BEYOND MYSELF
TO CHANGE SOMEONE'S DAY OR ENTIRE LIFE.

•••

I have watched my father on countless occasions reach into his wallet and bless some total stranger simply because his heart was telling him to. I've witnessed him encourage the guy behind the counter at a gas station, or the girl helping him with his dry cleaning, or the overwhelmed waitress at the restaurant.

Whether he realized it or not, he was teaching me to believe. He was teaching me to believe that I can and should be led by the Holy Spirit—to believe that meeting the needs of others is one of the greatest joys I can experience. He was teaching me to believe that it truly takes only a few minutes of reaching beyond myself to change someone's day or entire life.

I'm convinced that the most valuable times we shared as a family were the mornings before school spent around the breakfast table. That is where we received Communion together nearly every day.

What were my parents doing as my sister and I sat there with our broken cracker and Dixie cup of grape juice? They were teaching us to believe. They were teaching a little boy and girl that there is nothing more powerful on this planet than the blood of Jesus. They were demonstrating before us what it looks like, sounds like, and even feels like to be a believer in the broken body and spilled blood of Jesus. I am a believer today because they taught me how to be one. And I thank God that my father was man enough to lead his family and teach his kids how to believe.

But not all of us have had an earthly father around as a good role model. Not all of our fathers taught us to believe. So, for all of us who believe, we have some other wonderful role models. Abraham is a spiritual father to all of us who have faith in Jesus Christ. We can model his belief and obedience. Any of the heroes of the faith in Hebrews 11 are great examples. But most of all, we aspire to be more like Jesus. And what did Jesus say? "If you have seen Me, you have seen the Father."

So this time, what you'd put on your name tag is up to you, but I would encourage you to think of how it would impact your life if you walked around bearing the name of your Father for everyone to see—walked around as He would, doing what His Son would, and believing as your spiritual father and role model, Abraham, would.

"Hello. My name is <u>MY FATHER'S CHILD</u>" would be a good choice.

When we think like this—that we bear our Father's name out into the world—it can remind us how to behave. We emulate Jesus, who did nothing that He didn't see the Father do. This should be our identity—as sons and daughters of our Father.

Even when those around us cannot see God, we can bring Him honor by representing Him to our world. We can show the world our Father by learning to be like Him.

As you get up from reading this book, realize whose name you bear.

I would think by now you are beginning to pick up on the pattern of this book. I am writing because I want people to be quick to recognize God when they see Him. I want there to be less confusion and more certainty regarding His character, His will, and His ways.

Maybe God's moving is too subtle for some to pick up on and recognize, but I think if we could see over into the realm of the spirit, we might find God standing there with a name tag on. You can't get much clearer than that.

But if you are taking inventory of life and it seems that you never witness God's involvement in the affairs of men, I am telling you the quickest way to turn that around is for *you* to be the way He gets involved.

•••

EVEN WHEN THOSE AROUND US
CANNOT SEE GOD, WE CAN BRING HIM HONOR
BY REPRESENTING HIM TO OUR WORLD.

•••

You never see the mercy of God in action? Go be merciful. There. God just got involved, and He did it through you. He said that He would be a father to the fatherless. How is He going to do that? Through you. Take what He has taught you, through others, and begin to dish it out to the world you live in. You will soon become an eyewitness to the nature of God being revealed to humanity.

Then, if I've seen you, I've seen the Father.

A Word to Fathers

I went for a walk one evening before I first shared this message, "Have You Seen My Father?" I was just praying in the spirit, and I know that I know the Lord told me something for fathers who may be reading this who realize that they have failed to teach their children to believe.

•••

I DON'T NEED TO CARRY THE CARE.
HE IS CARRYING IT FOR ME.

•••

Maybe they didn't do such a great job, or they're having problems with a son or daughter. Maybe they knew and didn't do it, or maybe they've come to Christ only after having raised their children and now see what they could have taught them.

Listen, THE Father is saying one word to you right now: Mercy. There is mercy for your mistakes. There is mercy for the ways you have missed it. Receive His mercy, then show it to your children.

Maybe you need mercy *from* them. Go before your Father and receive it from Him first. Then cast the care of everything else on Him, because He cares for you (1 Peter 5:7). I used to read that thinking that I could give God all my cares because He cares *about* me. And of course that is true. But now, in addition to that concept, I like to read it with the emphasis on the word *for*. I cast my cares on Him because He cares *for* me. In other words, I don't need to carry the care, He is carrying it *for* me.

Fathers, He has already taken upon Himself the cares of this world, which include what you may have done wrong with your kids. Though it may challenge your pride to do so, cast the care on Him. Our God is faithful and knows how to restore families. It took Him several thousand years to get His family restored back to Him. Yours won't take nearly that long.

Fathers have a special mandate from God to represent Him; they have a responsibility that is somehow different because God identifies Himself as a Father. So I challenge you to begin living with this today.

Sit down with your sons or daughters. Find scriptures that will help strengthen their lives and their belief in God. Teach them to read the Bible. Teach them what it is to believe in Communion. Teach them what it means to believe that you're born again and you love the Lord. Teach them about their place of authority. Introduce them to God Almighty. Set the standard high for them, and teach them about mercy at the same time.

Teach your sons and daughters to believe. There is no greater legacy to leave them than that of a believer in the Lord Jesus Christ.

•••

FATHERS HAVE A SPECIAL MANDATE FROM GOD TO REPRESENT HIM.

•••

Let me ask you a question: Would any good father in his right mind withhold any good thing from his child if it were within his power to give it?

Wait—don't answer that. Let Jesus answer it. He said in Matthew 7:11, "If you then, being evil, know how to give good gifts to your children, how much more will your Father who is in heaven give good things to those who ask Him!"

Our heavenly Father is a giver! He proved His love for this world by giving us everything, including His only Son.

You can see that there has been confusion surrounding this concept of God through the ages. Many see Him as a taker of life, but that's not who He is. Your Father is the giver of all life, and Jesus came so that we could have that life.

Do you believe that? Do you believe that He is the One who gave health and healing?

Let's take a look at God our healer. Together, we're going to see what God's Word has to say when God introduces Himself to you as God, the One who heals you.

SECTION V

YOUR HEALER

Chapter Thirteen

THEY GOT WHAT THEY CAME FOR

I have some friends who help pastor a church in Aspen, Colorado, and they have taught some amazing messages regarding the character of God. Like us, they're endeavoring to go to deeper levels of understanding and insight into God's will and His ways.

One of my friends drew attention to a lady in the audience one day when he was teaching. He asked the congregation how many of them knew Yvette, who was sitting there in the front row. Many raised their hands. He then asked how many knew her as Yvette, the mother of little Tristan, who is a child in their church. Still, many raised their hands. He also brought up the fact that Yvette was a talented piano player. Most of the congregation was aware of that as she had often played in their church services.

But then he asked, "How many of you know her as Yvette, the concierge?" Not many in the crowd knew that about her. He went on to explain Yvette had worked for some time in Aspen as a concierge at a hotel there and knew just about everything there was to know about the town. With her knowledge of Aspen, she was able to help just about anyone with anything that guest may have needed to know about local eating, shopping, hot spots, etc.

His point was that many people knew her name and that she was a mother, and a piano player, but few knew about her professional life. People in that church could know Yvette for years, but if they didn't know that part of her character, then that part of who she was may never impact their lives.

•••

You CAN'T HAVE FAITH FOR
SOMETHING You DON'T KNOW To BE TRUE.

•••

"Because I know this about her," my friend said, "I have called on her many times to help me find a good place to eat, great shopping, even a place to stay when I was new in town."

He used this as an illustration that I found both simple and profound about why it's important to know all we can about God— His character, will, and ability. There may be those who have accepted Jesus as their Savior because they heard it was God's will for them to be saved. But they have lived the rest of their lives in the torment of fear, not knowing what God's Word says about His promise of protection and freedom from fear for those who call on Him.

This is true of all the many wonderful facets of God's character that He desires to show to those who will receive them by faith.

But you can't have faith for something you don't know to be true. Remember, faith deals not with the unknown, only the unseen. If you don't know the promises of God, then you can't yet have faith for them.

"Everyone who calls on the name of the Lord will be saved." But how can they call on him to save them unless they believe in him? And how can they believe in him if they have never heard about him? And how can they hear about him unless someone tells them? (Romans 10:13-14, NLT).

Of course my friend couldn't cover the entire nature of God in one message, and we can't do it in one book. But we can take our time and study one facet of His goodness at a time.

My friend's message that day was about that part of God's character revealed in Exodus 15:26: *"I am the Lord who heals you."* I want to turn our attention now to the same thing, so let's look together at the aspect of God's character as our healer.

•••

HIS NAME IS THE LORD WHO HEALS YOU.

•••

Hello. My Name Is Your Healer.

Did you know that He is the Lord who heals you? He's not the God who puts sickness on you. Not the one killing people with cancer or some other awful disease. He said, "I am the Lord who heals you." In other words, "Hello. My name is your Healer." His name is the One who took sickness away from the midst of you. His name is the Word who was sent and healed you. His name is the Lord who heals you—that's His name.

I told you we would be attacking confusion in the Body of Christ, and this is a place where we've really gotten mixed up. Not only are we confused regarding God's willingness to heal, but we've even fought word wars and split churches and families apart on this topic. It's amazing that something that seems so self-evident to me, that God wants His children well, could cause such division. But strife and confusion always walk hand in hand (see James 3:16), and when it comes to healing, the Body has its share of both regarding healing.

I've never seen this more clearly than I did recently when I watched a friend of mine fight a very personal battle with sickness and disease. However, she wasn't the one who was sick. She was close to someone who had unexpectedly become ill with a terrible disease that put him in the emergency room several times in the course of only a few months.

The boldness of the Spirit of God rose up in her throughout this struggle for her friend's life, and she began to confidently declare scripture after scripture that spelled out God's willingness to heal. She got her hands on every teaching she could find that talked about the power of God to heal, and she played them over and over and over.

...

FAITH BEGINS WHERE
THE WILL OF GOD IS KNOWN.

...

She is not the kind of person to force anything on *anyone,* but God seemed to be impressing on her that she was in this guy's life to help him live and not die. She continued to encourage him to read the Bible and books on healing, and to listen to CDs, to help get the principles about God's will to heal into his head and heart.

But his response was unenthusiastic at best. She began to see a major difference in the way they viewed God, and it took a toll on the relationship. Finally, when she (lovingly) confronted him about it with the truth of the Word of God, he told her that she was grossly misinterpreting Scripture and that he would never give the devil credit for something *God* was doing in his life.

When she told me that, it was like someone had punched me in the stomach. It hurt me to think that someone could lay blame or give credit to God for something so devilish as the disease that was ravaging his body.

Her friend is a Christian who loves God very much, but he has not yet come to see this part of the character and nature of our Father. And if you don't know this about God, how can you ever receive this from Him? You can't. Faith begins where the will of God is known. And where is the first place we go to find out His will? We run to His Word.

I Am *Is*

As I mentioned earlier in the book, one phrase in a verse of Scripture handily outlines our responsibility when it comes to God: "Without faith it is impossible to please God" (Hebrews 11:6, NIV). Without faith it is what? Impossible to please Him. Why? The rest of the verse tells us: "Because anyone who comes to him must believe that he exists and that he rewards those who earnestly seek him."

In this one verse of Scripture alone, it outlines my responsibility and yours when we come to God. First of all, we recognize that without faith we are nowhere near pleasing to Him. It is impossible to please Him without faith. Why would that be? Because it pleases Him to work in our lives, and faith is the only way we open that door to Him.

In the previous section, we talked about Abraham's belief—the standard of believing in which we take the Word of God and make our world fit His Word, rather than trying to make His Word fit our world. That's what faith is.

If you'll remember, the writer of Hebrews goes on to define faith after this verse about faith pleasing God. You'll remember he brings definition and form to this word *faith,* and he says those who come to God must do two things—or more specifically, must *believe* two things—that He exists and that He rewards.

So as we put it simply when talking about God's goodness, faith believes two things: God is and God gives. Not only do you believe that you're talking to the Creator of the universe—the Creator of heaven and earth, the Giver of life—you are confident that there is someone on the other end of the line who wants what's best for you. God's saying, "If you diligently seek Me, I will reward you."

This is not just a New Testament concept. In Psalm 37:4, David writes, "Delight yourself also in the Lord, and He shall give you the desires of your heart." Some have taken this one-dimensionally, seeing only part of it. "Lord," they say, "this thing is a desire of my heart." This job, this house, this blessing, my healing—whatever it may be. It's a desire in your heart, and by delighting in Him and believing in Him, you trust that He will provide it. And this is wonderful—we do this, and rightly so.

...

INSTEAD OF SEEKING HEALING, WE MUST SEEK THE HEALER.

...

But let me ask you this: What if *He* were the desire of your heart? He said, "You delight yourself in Me, I will give you *the* desire of your heart." Well, it seems to me that when I delight myself in Him, then that's exactly what He is. "You are the desire of my heart. You're what I long for. You are what I'm alive for." And He will give you of Himself, which is the best blessing of all!

This is a vital change of perspective from those who simply seek stuff—instead of seeking the gifts, we must seek the Giver. Instead of seeking healing, we must seek the Healer.

What have we been reading from Hebrews 11:6? He is a rewarder of those who seek *Him*. If you are seeking something, the only suitable reward is to find what you are seeking. When you seek Him, He *is* your reward. Can you think of any blessing whatsoever that could not be found in God? No!

The Bible tells us that when He gave us Jesus, He also freely gave us all things. When He gave you Jesus, He gave you prosperity. When He gave you Jesus, He gave you peace of mind. When He gave you Jesus, He gave you healing.

That is the tenor of David's statements throughout the Psalms. "O God, You are my God," he says. "Early will I seek You." He was hungry for more of God in his life because this life doesn't satisfy him. "My soul thirsts for You," he goes on. "My flesh longs for You in a dry and thirsty land where there is no water" (Psalm 63:1).

If you study David's life at the time he wrote this, you find that he was going through some extremely rough times. When he wrote about thirsting in a dry land where there was no water, he was in the wilderness of Judah. There was literally nothing to eat or drink. Yet, even at a time he was thirsty and starving, his greatest hunger was for the presence of the Lord!

So faith is not only believing He exists, but it's believing He is so real that when I actively and aggressively pursue Him, He rewards me with...what? *Him.* He is my reward. He is what I'm looking for. He is what we're after.

What did Jesus say? "Seek the kingdom of God first, and everything else will be added to you at the right time." Don't worry about this stuff. You can line up cars and houses and money and everything else in a row, and it is *nothing* in and of itself. None of it compares to desiring and being rewarded with God Himself, poured out in your life.

For our part, we believe He exists and we pursue Him. We believe that He is, and we believe that He gives.

Daddy

Have you ever noticed how little girls can get whatever they want from their fathers? Some kids may get manipulative, but that's not what I'm talking about. There's a simple dynamic at work between a loving parent and child, and there's a key for us in that relationship.

Daddy's girl knows that when she has a need, she doesn't get it filled by being rebellious. She doesn't get Daddy's attention by throwing temper tantrums. She doesn't slam doors when she doesn't get what she wants or needs right away.

The key to getting what you want from Daddy, good little girls know, is crawling up in his lap, looking deep into his eyes, and saying…what? Saying how much she loves him.

"Daddy, I love you," she says. "I love you, Daddy." And his big daddy heart just melts. And Daddy says, "Whatever you want, honey." We've all seen it.

His heart of love is moved when she comes to him with her needs, wrapped in her love. So do you think that this father is put out by giving to her? Do you think he dreads it? Maybe, if she's being manipulative just to get what she wants. But if she really just does love Daddy and is now asking for something, how do you think he feels about delighting her? And do you think he'll give her something that's harmful to her, that he'll let her have something that will hurt her?

This thought left me wondering, is there a key like this in God's heart? Is there a key in delighting in the Lord and experiencing Him and also walking in the blessing of all that He has provided through Jesus?

The short answer is yes—yes there is. It's Hebrews 11:6. You get up in His lap and you say, "Father, I believe. I believe what You said. I believe who You are. I believe in every way You have ever introduced Yourself to me and everybody else on this earth. I found You in Your Word, and I believe Your Word. I seek You first, and I'm trusting you based on the integrity of

Your Word that You're going to meet my needs and give me the desires of my heart."

That's the key to this, and I want to look at several examples of people who came to Jesus and got exactly what they wanted—because that's what I'm looking for. I'm looking for that key. I want to know you can come to the Lord right away instead of walking around in the desert for forty years before you cooperate with His way of doing things.

So please understand that I am in no way suggesting that God is some kind of fairy godmother we just use to get what we want. I'm also not suggesting that by batting our eyelashes and trying really hard we can get Him to do what we want.

I am, however, talking about you and me coming to Him based on the authority and integrity of His Word, which tells us about His will and His desires. I'm talking about coming to Him based on the faith that we talked about earlier—that He is and that He rewards those who seek Him. I'm talking about coming to Him and asking for nothing more than the Bible already says is His will to give—for us to live healed and whole, all the days of our lives.

He's made it clear in His Word, if we'll bother to read it and get to know Him. So let's look a little more closely at the Lord our Healer.

Chapter Fourteen

BELIEVE. SAY. DO.

In Mark 5, we read the account of Jairus, one of the rulers of a local synagogue, who comes to Jesus. It says that when Jairus saw Jesus, he fell at His feet—that's important, so remember it for later—and said, "My little daughter lies at the point of death. Come and lay Your hands on her, that she may be healed, and she will live" (verse 23).

That last little bit is important too—"she will live." Now notice who said this; it wasn't Jesus. This was not a voice from on High. This was the man in need. This was the man who came to Jesus looking for something, needing something.

The next statement in the following verse has to be one of my favorite parts in Scripture. It simply says this: "So Jesus went with him." No questions asked. He doesn't ask the disciple carrying His day planner if they can fit it in, doesn't ask a bunch of questions, and doesn't give the guy a hard time for being the leader of a local synagogue. Jesus just went with him. I want that to be the story of my life. Don't you?

So what did Jairus do to get Jesus to go with him without so much as a word? I want to know what this man did—he got results. Evidently Jairus did something that Jesus liked.

Let's start by looking at what we know about Jairus. We read that he's a ruler of the synagogue, so he's a man with position. A man with authority. A little study into this shows that he wasn't necessarily the preacher of their synagogue; he may have been some sort of overseer—an administrator. He was probably known in the community, inside and outside of the synagogue, as a person of some status, reputation, and position.

Now what else do we know about the rulers of the synagogues, the religious people of that time? I think it's safe to say they were not founding members of the Jesus Christ Fan Club.

Jesus came on the scene with a new perspective, new teaching—changing all the rules, as we've noted before. He messed with their established order of things, because they only knew how to preach other men's opinions to the people. We have read multiple accounts of these men questioning where Jesus got His authority; they did this because He wasn't quoting another rabbi's teachings, as they did.

Instead, Jesus showed up all of the sudden and stood in a place of authority, saying, "God Himself says…" and then laid it out for them. So this is the climate of friction in which Jesus and these religious leaders lived with one another: They were clinging to their traditional teachings, and Jesus was a new radical, preaching with authority.

It's possible that Jairus would have been one of the former, trying to cling to their power base and authority. He was a man of reputation, of clout within the community. Regardless of Jairus' personal view of Jesus, I'm sure he associated with some of the religious leaders who were at least skeptical regarding Jesus.

But instead of standing on this power structure derived from the opinions of other men, Jairus doesn't let his position, reputation, or appearances stand in the way of recognizing something: His hope lay in going to Jesus.

Jairus tells us something about himself, because even with all the people who know him and where he stands within the community gathered around, Jairus makes a beeline for Jesus as soon as He gets off the boat.

I bet it looked something like this—Jesus has just stepped off the boat from coming across the lake, and there's already a crowd of people. It's a crowd that, I guarantee, knows Jairus from church.

•••

FAITH DROVE HIM TO FIND JESUS,
AND IT'LL DO THE SAME THING
FOR YOU AND ME.

•••

In the middle of this crowd gathered to see Jesus, somebody isn't being too concerned with social niceties. Somebody isn't being polite. Someone is pushing, forcing his way through the press of robed bodies standing by the lakeshore. The grumbles of people getting bumped and pushed to one side or another start near the back and then work forward, and heads begin to turn. Who is this rude man, this inconsiderate fellow who is pushing and shoving to get to the teacher, Jesus?

I imagine some eyes growing wide when those gathered around see who it is—Jairus, the normally calm-and-collected leader of the synagogue. It's the unruffled, dignified man who normally has it all together. The one who is in charge, who takes everyone else's crises and diffuses them.

With his forehead knit in concern, he's moving people aside and pushing his way to the front, until he gets to Jesus. In his moment of need, here's Jairus. He's probably dressed in his suit and tie for the day, probably got his golden name tag on that says, "Jairus, Ruler of the Synagogue." He comes pushing his way through, and then what does he do?

He falls at Jesus' feet.

Faith is about humbling yourself under the mighty hand of God. This man had a need, and he wasn't about to let something as small as a reputation stand between him and his little girl's life. Do you think he cared about his reputation? Do you think he cared about getting his suit dirty? Not if he was a good father, he didn't. Not if he's a man at all. Do you think he cared that in the last Rulers of the Synagogue meeting his contemporaries were talking about what to do about "the Jesus problem"? He didn't care about any of that.

Faith drove him to find Jesus, and it'll do the same thing for you and me.

• • •

FAITH PUSHES THROUGH AND
THEN DROPS TO ITS KNEES.

• • •

You might not have to push through a physical crowd, but it may be a crowd of circumstances or a crowd of disbelievers around you. You may have to push through your concerns and worries, your misgivings and doubts. You may have to push through the pages of that Bible, which starts out with some genealogies in the New Testament and forces you to dig through them until you find the promise God has for you—until you find that rhema word of God that's alive and breathing.

Jairus pushed his way through the crowd until he found the One who could help him, and then he fell, humble, at His feet. Your moment of need isn't the time for shaking your fist at God and saying, "Why me?" It's not the time for expressing anger to God and asking Him why He did this to you.

That's not faith.

Faith pushes through and then drops to its knees. Faith is humbling yourself under the mighty hand of God. Faith says, "God, thank You for the precious blood of Jesus that takes away my sins—the same blood He shed for my healing." Faith doesn't care how long you've been in your church. Faith doesn't care about what you think people might think of you if you asked for prayer. It doesn't care about any of it.

All faith knows is pushing through to the feet of Jesus and then falling humbly before Him.

Jairus' Three Steps of Faith

I realize I must be watchful when I say that there are "steps" that Jairus took in faith. Some may hear that and be tempted to turn what I say into a mechanical, lifeless procedure in hopes that it "makes" God do something for them. I do think, however, the word "steps" is the appropriate word.

Second Corinthians 5:7 says we *walk* by faith and not by sight. How do you walk? One *step* at a time. When you get out of your car and are headed for the front door, how do you arrive there? One step at a time. You don't sit in the car frustrated and confused as to why you are not already at the front door or inside on the couch. If that is where you want to be, then get up and take the appropriate steps to get there.

The walk of faith is the same way. You may be looking at where you are and desiring to be further down the road. Instead of being angry with God or disappointed in yourself because you are not already there, get up and take one step of faith. That's what Jairus did, and Jairus' walk of faith seems to be three steps long.

First, he cared less about what people thought of him than what it would take to get to the Healer. He didn't care about his reputation more than his daughter's life. He found Jesus. That is always step one.

Second, his faith was about humility. He didn't care if he had to get face-down in the dirt; he was going to present himself to Jesus and believe that Jesus was going to come with him that day. Since

Jesus was the only one with the answer, Jairus was committed that Jesus was going to accompany him that day.

Jairus' faith was about one more thing, and we read it when he says, "My little daughter lies at the point of death. Come and lay Your hands on her, that she may be healed, and she will live." When belief has taken hold of you down deep in your heart, the next thing it must do is *come out of your mouth*.

In a nutshell, faith is about believing it, saying it, and doing it.

That's what salvation is. You believe in your heart. You say with your mouth Jesus Christ is the Son of God, risen from the dead. And then you live like that. You believe it. You say it. You do it.

Believing something and saying what you believe are not two separate things. They are simply two sides of the same thing. And what thing is that? Faith.

Faith is making a whole life out of this simple process. If I see it in the Word, I believe it. I believe it, so I'm going to say it out loud. And if I don't want to make a liar out of myself, I am going to do what I say. I'm going to do what I see the Word tells me to do.

And that's just what this man did. And Jesus went with him. No, Jairus did not have the written Word of God in New and Old Testament the way you and I have it today, but he did have the Word made manifest and dwelling among them. Whether he realized it or not, when he put his trust in Jesus, he was putting his trust in the Word of God.

The *Jesus*

Jesus is going with Jairus, and they head for his house amid a throng of people. And we pick up the story of a woman in that group of people.

This woman has a problem—she's been bleeding for years, and she's tried everything. Doctors, chiropractors, nutritionists—who knows what all she tried. Not only did none of it work, but in fact, her condition actually only got worse. And in going to all these people, she has spent a fortune.

But then things suddenly look up. Jesus gets off the boat.

It says, "When she heard about Jesus, she came behind Him in the crowd and touched His garment" (Mark 5:27). This is important—when she hears about Him, she comes. The Greek language literally translates to say that she had heard things concerning *the* Jesus. She had heard about the miracles of healing and deliverance Jesus had been doing, and she knew that if she could just get close enough—could just even touch the fringe of His robe—she would be healed.

That's faith. She knows that if she can just get to the Healer, she'll get what she needs. After she touches Him, it says, "Immediately the fountain of her blood was dried up, and she felt in her body that she was healed of the affliction" (Mark 5:29).

Jesus is aware of this—He knows what has happened. It says that He knew that healing power had gone out of Him, and He turns around to see who it was. Jesus says, "Who touched Me?"

The disciples probably look at Him sideways, because He's in the middle of a crowd of people, and they ask Him, "Don't you see the people crowding against You? How can You ask who touched You?"

The Bible tells us, "And He looked around to see her who had done this thing. But the woman, fearing and trembling, knowing what had happened to her, came and fell down before Him and told Him the whole truth" (Mark 5:32-33).

And Jesus says to her, "Daughter, your faith has made you well. Go in peace, and be healed of your affliction" (Mark 5:34).

This lady and Jairus share similar stories, and they have the same result. They pushed in to Jesus, and they got what they came for.

Now what do we know about this woman? She'd spent everything she had, and her problem had only worsened. We read that she was drained physically and emotionally. We don't know who she was in her community or what people thought of her, but we know she had something in common with Jairus. She had a need.

When she heard about Jesus, something different happened inside of her. Faith began to rise. Notice the source of faith was from nothing more than hearing about Jesus. She'd heard about the blind eyes seeing and deaf ears hearing. She'd heard about straightened limbs. She'd heard about the dead being given life again.

So when she heard that this same Man was there, she went to Him with one thing on her mind—just touching His cloak.

Romans 10:17 tells us that faith comes by hearing and hearing by the Word of God. You've probably heard that one before. But a little closer look at the original Greek language reveals that Paul said here that faith comes by hearing and hearing "the word about Christ." The *Wuest Translation* says, "So then, faith is out of the source of that which is heard, and that which is heard (the message) is through the agency of the Word concerning Christ."

When you hear the Word concerning Christ, the same thing will happen in you. Your faith in Him will begin to rise. (This is why it is so important to be in a place where you are constantly hearing the good news of Jesus Christ. Listen to teachers and preachers who will tell you about Jesus!)

A little research reveals that this issue of blood had another connotation: According to Jewish law, this flow of blood would make her "unclean." She shouldn't have been in the crowd, brushing up against people. She was breaking the rules, not caring about her reputation or what people thought of her, just as Jairus did. Her faith was about nonconformity—it didn't care about what the rules or other people said about her. It didn't care about her reputation.

When she heard about Jesus, she believed in Him. But what else did she do? She said to herself that she only had to *touch* Him and she'd be made well.

Not only did she say it, we find again in the Greek text that she kept on saying it to herself and others as she pressed through the crowd. Interestingly, the word translated "be made whole" is actually the Greek word *sozo,* meaning salvation. Her salvation that day wasn't to be only physical, but spiritual as well.

When she heard about Jesus, she came behind Him in the crowd and touched Him. When she believed in Him, she got up, broke the rules, and got in the street to find Him. She dug her way through the same crowd that Jairus was in—pushed her way around until she got close enough to touch this Man.

She believed it. She said it. She did it.

And when He turned to face her, what did she do? She fell on her face before Him. She humbled herself.

Every time, faith is humility. Faith is the recognition that, had it not been for the grace of God through Jesus, we would stay sick.

But then comes grace. Then comes mercy. And with faith and humility, you step out of what you deserve and into what He gave you.

Grace is God saying, "I have purchased your healing with the stripes of My Son, Jesus." But faith is your part in the conversation. And by faith you say, "I'll take it. Thank You for such a wonderful gift."

We've never done anything worthy of His healing and blessing, but *He said* we were worthy—worth His stripes, His blood, His nail-pierced hands and side. Worth His death. You are worthy. *Because He said so.*

Jesus says we are worth it, and faith chooses to believe it. It chooses to say it. It chooses to live it. Just as Jairus and this woman did.

Let's look at their belief a little more deeply.

Chapter Fifteen

STOP THE NOISE

Back to Jairus. You see, while all this was happening with the woman, things at Jairus' household appeared to be getting a lot worse. Literally while Jesus was talking to this woman, one of Jairus' servants came up to them and told him some bad news.

"Your daughter is dead. Why trouble the Teacher any further?" (Mark 5:35).

The subtext here may have been something like this: "You fool, you ruined your reputation acting like a common beggar trying to get to this guy, and now by associating with Him, you've probably lost your job. And it was for nothing—it's too late." It was all for nothing, he's saying.

But Jesus hears it too. It says, "Ignoring what they said, Jesus told the synagogue ruler, 'Don't be afraid; just believe'" (verse 36, NIV).

Just believe. It's what He was after from the woman at the well; it's what He was after from Jairus; and it is what He desires from countless others, including you and me.

Belief.

Interestingly, this is the first thing Jesus says to Jairus—*"Don't be afraid; just believe."* I picture it like this: The servant comes and delivers that bad news to Jairus. And Jesus turns around, locks eyes with Jairus, and grabs him by that expensive suit he wears to the office.

Now that He's gotten his attention, Jesus says, "You came to Me for a reason—if you want Me to do it, you can't allow fear in. There is no room for fear, only belief. That faith that you brought when you came running to Me, that's the only thing there's room for. Jairus, nothing has changed. Before, she was almost dead. Now, she's dead. OK. *I'm still Jesus.* Only believe."

I can almost see Jairus looking into Jesus' eyes, choking his fear down and mastering it with the belief that brought him there. "OK," he says, nodding but never quite taking his eyes off Jesus. "OK, let's go."

...

SLAM THE DOOR ON DOUBT.

...

And they go on to Jairus' house, with Jesus bringing only Peter, James, and John with them. At the house, people are wailing loudly over the dead girl. And Jesus says to them, "Why make this commotion and weep? The child is not dead, but sleeping" (verse 39).

And what do they do? These people, who a moment before were wailing and weeping, *laugh* at Him! It says in verse 40, "And they ridiculed Him. But when He had put them all outside, He took the father and the mother of the child, and those who were with Him, and entered where the child was lying."

They laugh at him, but Jesus exemplifies faith. Real faith doesn't care if people laugh at it. Jesus doesn't care about His reputation or how people take what He says. But he doesn't need

Jairus and his wife—and the disciples—hearing these people, so
He throws them out.

"You want to doubt? Fine. You can doubt out there." Then He
slams the door in their faces! He gets their doubt out of the picture, so that Jairus can only hear the voice of faith and not doubt.

You and I have to do the same thing. When we come to the
Lord in a moment of need like this, we have to shut out every
other voice. Slam the door on doubt.

My parents demonstrated this to me when I was growing up. If
I got sick—which didn't happen often, but every other year or so
I did come down with something—they didn't handle it the way it
seemed to me most other parents did.

Now, when the kids I went to school with came back after being out sick a few days, they would tell us that it wasn't so bad—
they just lay around and watched TV.

That always perplexed me, because that wasn't how it was for
me. We got to the point in my house that we thought twice about
saying, "My stomach hurts," because even if it was the middle of
the night, the sheets would come off and the lights come on. It
was time to get out your Bible and books and tapes on healing—
especially those my grandparents had made.

•••

SHUT OUT EVERY VOICE OTHER THAN FAITH.

•••

My parents didn't handle sickness lying down—they fought it.
And we fought it with them! Saying something like, "I don't feel
like it" was like cussing to them; you just didn't do it.

We shut out every other voice. There was no TV on when I was
sick, and they reminded me, "It's not time to turn that thing on.
Neither *The Price Is Right, Gomer Pyle, Gilligan's Island,* nor any
of the other midday TV viewing options died for you. None of

those took stripes for your healing. None of those things bled the ground red for you.

"None of those things rose from the dead out of hell itself so that you could be healed."

So why would you want that voice distracting you from the voice of faith? They taught me to shut out every voice other than faith.

And that's what Jesus did. He shut those so-called mourners out, with their laughter and their ridicule, because He didn't care what they thought. He closed the door on anything that wasn't faith.

It says,

> The crowd laughed at him. But he made them all leave, and he took the girl's father and mother and his three disciples into the room where the girl was lying. Holding her hand, he said to her, "Talitha koum," which means "Little girl, get up!" And the girl, who was twelve years old, immediately stood up and walked around! They were overwhelmed and totally amazed (verses 40-42, NLT).

Jairus got what he needed from Jesus. Whatever he did, he got the results he was looking for—his little girl was alive and not dead.

How do you and I get the results we're looking for? Do the exact same thing.

The woman with the issue of blood got exactly what she needed—nothing short of total healing. How do we experience this as well? Do exactly what she did.

Please note again that I am not giving you some mechanical approach to receiving from God. Remember, you just want to get from the car to the front door, but there are steps involved, and

I'm simply telling you what will happen when genuine faith rises up in you. This is what it will look like, sound like, and act like. Also, in the other sections, I've given you steps you can follow to help you get started, and these steps are no different.

You come running in faith and humble yourself under the mighty hand of God. You look in His Word and say, "I believe this. I'm going to say it, and I'm going to do it." Then you do it. You shut out everything that isn't faith, and focus on God.

When you experience something that's beyond your experience, you pass beyond your own understanding. You have no choice but to rely on Him—to turn to Him humbly and in faith, believing that He has done for you all He promised to do. Tell Him, "I'm going to believe it. I'm going to say it, and I'm going to do it."

Healing for your body is a part of the finished work of Jesus upon the cross, but you must receive it. God doesn't force things on anyone. He set before us life and death, blessing and cursing. Choose life.

So here are your three steps: Believe it. Say it. Do it.

Faith Buddies

Let's take a look at one more individual—or rather, a handful of them. The crowd that surrounded Jesus when Jairus and the woman with the issue of blood approached Him wasn't unique; in fact, it seemed to be the norm.

In fact, there's such a crowd that in one instance, these guys who are carrying their friend—who is paralyzed—can't get into the house where He's staying. He's busy preaching the Word, and it's so packed that these people can't get in with their friend who needs healing. It says,

And when they could not come near Him because of the crowd, they uncovered the roof where He was. So when they had broken through, they let down the bed on which the paralytic was lying. When Jesus saw their faith, He said to the paralytic, "Son, your sins are forgiven you" (Mark 2:4-5).

Jesus saw their faith—faith that didn't care that He was in the middle of preaching, that they were potentially offending people in line ahead of them.

I like to imagine the back story for this guy and his four friends. I wonder if he wasn't always paralyzed—maybe something happened. They were all skiing together and he got hurt, and now they all feel responsible. Or maybe it was a work-related injury, like at a building site or something. Or maybe it was a freak, high-speed donkey accident, and he wasn't wearing his seat belt!

Whatever happened, he's got these four roommates—young guys just starting their careers; and while they love him and would do anything for him, he's needy.

Ever since "the incident," he's said things like, "Oh, hey buddy, while you're up, can you give me a Coke? I would, but I'm paralyzed. Thanks." Or, "Hey man, can you hand me the remote? I can't reach it. It's right there. I would...but I'm paralyzed. Sorry. I can't. Thanks."

And I'm imagining this has been going on for quite some time in this house; these friends, they love their friend and would do anything for the guy. They talk in hushed tones, "Bless his heart. Terrible accident. We just want to help him, but we've heard enough about the paralyzed thing. We're all living for ourselves and trying to meet his need too. This is getting ridiculous."

And he probably could do some things for himself, but sometimes he doesn't—he doesn't work for it, because he knows his friends are there to help him. He knows they'll take care of it for him, so he doesn't try on his own.

Clearly I am taking some artistic liberties here, but the truth is that sickness can be insidious like that, taking away your initiative and getting you to almost *like* being sick because it affords you some luxury or notoriety.

It can be hard on your flesh to stand and fight when all you want to do is lie there. And it's sometimes easier to let someone else do things for you instead of struggling against the doubt and other voices. You've got to be careful, because sickness and other afflictions—whatever apparent positives they may get for you— are not the will of God.

So maybe these friends understand that. They know it's easier for this guy to let them help him all the time because they love him.

But then they hear that Jesus is in town, and they hold an all-roommate meeting and decide to do something about it.

It's the same thing that happened to Jairus and to the woman with the issue of blood—they heard about Jesus. These guys heard He was in town, and they said, "This is it. This is what he needs. Grab one side of the bed, and I'll get the other!"

We don't know how this man felt about this; he might have even objected. "Put me down, man! I'm paralyzed! Don't...don't do that! You'll drop me! What's going on? What are you doing?"

And being guys, they would've said something lovingly, like, "Shut up, man. We're taking you to see Jesus. Just relax, would ya?"

So they get to the house, and it's packed—people everywhere. Maybe this guy was like, "Look guys. Too many people. We can't get in. Nice thought. Let's just go home, and you can get me a Coke."

But they aren't to be deterred. "No way. We came all this way, carrying your sorry self. We're getting you healed, man—today! You are *walking* home, son."

There's no room, and they stand around talking about it for a moment until one of them, maybe a roofer, looks up. "You thinking what I'm thinking?" Heads nod. "Let's do this thing."

So they drag him up there, maybe bumping on the way up the stairs. "Hey! Guys, stop it! I'm paralyzed, watch it!" But they get him up there.

And Jesus is busy preaching in the living room, and He can hear people stomping around on the roof. Maybe He gets this knowing smile on His face, and He's looking up, smiling at them, when they pry enough of the roof away to get a look at Him down there.

"Oh, hello. Sorry to interrupt..."

Faith doesn't care about the roof; the roofer roommate will fix it later. Faith doesn't care about interrupting; Jesus is smiling at them as one of them pokes his head down through the hole they make. Faith presses through, digs through what's in the way.

•••

THEIR FAITH WELLED UP INSIDE
AND DREW SOMETHING OUT OF THEM.

•••

I don't know how you would lower a guy through a hole in the roof, so maybe they just kind of plop him down in front of Jesus— drop him, basically. He's about to get healed anyway, right?

And Jesus sees their faith. He doesn't have to perceive it or pick up on it. He sees it; their faith just cuts a hole in the roof to get this guy to Him! They're maybe hanging their heads down into the hole they made, all four of them, and are like, "You're Jesus, right? We were wondering, would you please do something about this joker? He's paralyzed, and he's gotta be healed. He needs it. *We* need it."

They didn't care what anyone thought of them, including their friend. They knew that Jesus had the answer for him, and for them, and they believed that He would turn that situation around. Their faith inspired them to something great in getting him there, and Jesus reacted to it with something greater—healing.

Their faith, welling up inside them, drew something out of them. They heard Jesus was in town, believed He could help their friend, and then acted by bringing their buddy to Him.

This guy had faith buddies—people so interested and involved in his life that they'd look to his real need and then seek to get it met, whatever it took. We all need people like that, and we must *be* people like that.

We don't need people that fawn over us in our sickness: "Oh, you poor baby." No, we need people who remind us what God's Word says about healing for our bodies. We need people who remind us how healed we are because of the price that was paid. People who remind us that the blood of Jesus still speaks for us, who remind us of the stripes that He took on His back so we could be healed, and that we serve the God who took sickness away from us. We need people in our lives who bring it to our memory that He sent His Word and healed us, and that He always proves Himself faithful.

Everybody needs a faith buddy, but it's important to be that person in turn for others.

In a world where people often ask, "Where was God? Where is God?" I want them to know that they can find Him in the lives of Christian believers. I want to be a part of a group of people who don't just associate with God because of a name or label but in the character and product of our lives.

It's one thing to lock into and focus exclusively on the Word of God for the healing of your body, but it is another thing entirely to join someone else in believing for their healing. When you do, you have just become a part of God revealing His love and goodness toward that person.

When you do, He uses your mouth to say, "Hello. My name is God your Healer."

I Believe. Help My Unbelief.

A lot has been said through the years about "how" to receive healing. Countless preachers and teachers have made books and sermons galore, and many of them I'm sure are very helpful.

But I don't want you to focus on the "how" here as much as I want to look at the "who." Fix your eyes on Jesus.

Colossians says that He is the visible image of the invisible God. In other words, every word Jesus spoke was God the Father speaking to mankind. Every action Jesus took was God's express will and purpose for the earth. In fact, Jesus never did or said anything that was outside the will of His Father. Every blind eye opened, every lame leg made whole, every leper cleansed, and every dead person raised was God revealing His will to heal to all men for all time.

Over and over again, the Gospels relay examples of the healing power that flowed through Jesus to anyone who came to Him in faith.

•••

IT'S NOT ABOUT WHAT HE CAN DO.
IT'S ABOUT WHAT YOU CAN BELIEVE.

•••

If you are going to receive the manifestation of God's healing power in your body, you must first hear of His will to heal you. The Word is filled with scriptures about God's desire to heal, and many of these have even been recorded so you can listen to them. But whatever you do, hear the Word about healing and get it inside you.

Second, you must recognize and *believe* that He is the healer. In Mark 6, Jesus could do no mighty works in His hometown of Nazareth because His friends and family did not recognize Him for who He was. They did not believe that He was who He said

He was. Through their unbelief, they limited what Jesus could do in their lives.

Does it surprise you to think that you might be the one limiting God's power in your life? You might think, *Well, I thought God was God, and He can do anything.* God *is* God, and He *can* do anything. But not everything is up to what God can do.

Don't get mad at me here. Stay with me, and I will prove to you what I am talking about.

In Mark 9, a man brought his son to Jesus to be delivered from an evil spirit. The Bible says that when that evil spirit saw Jesus, it threw the child into a violent convulsion, and he fell to the ground writhing and foaming at the mouth.

Desperate, the boy's father says to Jesus, "Have mercy on us and help us, if you can" (verse 22, NLT).

I love Jesus' response in the next verse. He says, "What do you mean, 'If I can'?... Anything is possible if a person believes" (NLT).

Did you catch that? This boy's miracle was not dependent on Jesus' ability. It depended on the presence of faith. Of course Jesus can. The *New King James Version* says it like this: "If you can believe, all things are possible to him who believes" (verse 23).

It's not about what He can do. It's about what you can believe.

My friend, believing is simply a choice. You can believe anything. Some people say, "Well, I just can't believe that God would do that for me."

No. You can believe it. You just choose not to.

When Jesus told the boy's father that all things were possible if he would believe, the man shouted out, "Lord, I believe, help my unbelief!" (Mark 9:24). In other words, "I believe it. And if there is any part of me that doesn't believe, help me get rid of it!"

God is so merciful and kind toward us. By his own admission, this man was weak in faith, but he was not void of it. He cried out to the Lord for help, and that is exactly what Jesus did. He helped.

Can you see how powerful it is to know what you believe?

We're looking at the true nature of God, not so you can deduce ways of getting what you want out of Him, but so that this revelation gets down deep in you and becomes your new way of believing.

If you've never before heard that God is a good God who wants you healed, then it's time to change your thinking and grab onto that promise by faith. You may be dealing with symptoms in your body right this very moment. If so, it's time to shut out that voice of doubt, just as Jesus did with the mourners in Jairus' house, and decide not to be influenced by what you see or feel. Those things are subject to change.

Allow what you have heard about Jesus Christ, the One who took stripes upon His back to purchase your healing, to rise up big in you. If you believe that what He said and did is true, then say it—out loud, the third step: "I was healed, and I am healed by the stripes of Jesus."

"Do I really have to say it?" you may be asking.

To that I respond, if you believed it you couldn't *help* but say it. Second Corinthians 4:13 says, "And since we have the same spirit of faith, according to what is written, 'I believed and therefore I spoke,' we also believe and therefore speak."

Paul goes on in verse 16 to say, "Therefore we do not lose heart."

Don't quit. Don't ever quit believing the Word of God. Don't draw back, don't retreat, and don't lose heart. Verse 18 says that we do not look at things that are seen, but at the things which are unseen. The things that are seen are temporary, and the unseen things are eternal.

Does that sound familiar? Faith doesn't deal with the unknown, only the unseen.

Once you have established what—or in whom—you believe, do exactly what we have seen in the Word: Believe it. Say it. Act on it. Don't just be a hearer of the Word, be a doer of the Word you hear. As you do, you will walk in deeper revelations of the character of God than you ever have before.

I have included an appendix at the end of the book that has various scriptures dealing with God's healing power, which is available to anyone who will believe it. Take time to look at them and make the decision that you are going to believe what you read.

This is who God is. God is **YOUR HEALER.**

I know this is a lot to process, and that there is no way I, or anyone, could communicate the full nature of God in a few chapters of one book. The truth is, we need help. We need help in understanding and comprehending His love, mercy, and authority in our lives. We need help in seeing Him as our Father and our healer. And for everything that is not talked about in this book and everything that is still beyond what I know, I need His help.

I want to show you that He hasn't left us solely responsible for figuring this all out. Help is on the way.

SECTION VI
HELP WANTED

Chapter Sixteen

FAITH IN REVERSE

I want to talk more about hearing God's voice—and discerning it. How often does God speak to us far more clearly than we give Him credit for, but we don't hear Him or don't know it's Him? How often are we expecting Him in the wind, the earthquake, or the fire, when in fact He's using a still, small voice?

Remember the Samaritan woman at the well, whom we read about in the first section? What was Jesus doing with her?

He was endeavoring to solicit belief. He was making statements that required ears to hear, trying different tactics to get through to her. She gets close...sort of. She thinks He's a prophet, and she tries to make it a religious discussion—she tries debating religion with the Son of God! She has no idea to whom she's speaking until He reveals Himself.

Hello. My name is God.

Jesus spent the whole conversation trying to solicit belief. He was doing everything He could short of slapping on His name tag and proclaiming Himself (which He ended up having to do anyway). Why?

In a sense, it's simple. Perhaps you've picked up on it already. Jesus was trying to inspire *faith* in this woman, as He is in you and me. It takes no faith to believe God is there after He's had to turn on a blazing neon sign to get through to us. When He shows up with His name tag glowing its brightest, greatest glory, it doesn't take any faith to know He is there.

But how did He reveal Himself to Elijah? The still, small voice—not the obvious, in-your-face signs we might have expected. How did Jesus approach this woman? Incognito.

So how do you think He shows up in our lives most of the time?

•••

IT TAKES NO FAITH TO BELIEVE
GOD IS THERE AFTER HE'S HAD TO
TURN ON A BLAZING NEON SIGN
TO GET THROUGH TO US.

•••

He shows up every day through His mercy, even in our next breath. He shows up through His authority as our Father and the guarantor of our covenant. He shows up when the healing He bought and paid for becomes a reality in our physical bodies after we dare to take Him at His Word.

It's our role in this to be spiritually mature and to look for Him in our everyday lives—lives where the neon God-lights aren't blazing to reveal His presence, earthquakes haven't shaken the house from its foundation, flash-fires haven't coursed through the living room, and no hurricanes have messed up our hair.

You went to sleep sick and woke up healed. *God is on the scene.*

You told the devourer to get off your finances, and that audit turned up a clean bill of health for your taxes. *God is on the scene.*

You got that promotion you wanted, or your kid got into the college he wanted to attend. *God is on the scene.*

And, by faith, you begin to recognize that God was on the scene even before you saw the physical manifestation. That is maturity. Why?

Because having faith requires patience, and the Scriptures promise that patience will make you perfect. That word *perfect* means "complete and mature." That is how you recognize the presence of God when it seems to everyone else that He is nowhere to be found. We've got to become quick to recognize Him—quick to see His attributes and presence in the everyday events of our lives.

That's our part: being mature Christians who know the voice of God.

Is That You, Lord?

Let's look at someone who heard God's voice and had to learn to discern it. You may be familiar with the story of Samuel. His mother, Hannah, couldn't get pregnant, so when she finally did, she was so grateful to God that she committed Samuel to His service. When he was still a little boy, she brought him to the temple, where he lived and ministered to the Lord under the direction of Eli, the priest.

Hannah saw Samuel when she brought him new clothes, and that was it! How would you like that, moms—seeing your little blessing from God once a year?

The rest of the time, Samuel lived and served in the house of the Lord. In fact, it says, "The boy Samuel grew up in the presence of the Lord" (1 Samuel 2:21, NIV). Let's pick up on Samuel's life at a key time—a pivotal point in his ministry to the Lord. It's when he was learning to hear from God.

Now in those days messages from the Lord were very rare, and visions were quite uncommon. One night Eli, who was almost blind by now, had gone to bed. The lamp of God had not yet gone out, and Samuel was sleeping in the Tabernacle near the Ark of God. Suddenly the Lord called out, "Samuel!" "Yes?" Samuel replied. "What is it?" He got up and ran to Eli. "Here I am. Did you call me?" "I didn't call you," Eli replied. "Go back to bed." So he did. Then the Lord called out again, "Samuel!" Again Samuel got up and went to Eli. "Here I am. Did you call me?" "I didn't call you, my son," Eli said. "Go back to bed." Samuel did not yet know the Lord because he had never had a message from the Lord before. So the Lord called a third time, and once more Samuel got up and went to Eli. "Here I am. Did you call me?" Then Eli realized it was the Lord who was calling the boy. So he said to Samuel, "Go and lie down again, and if someone calls again, say, 'Speak, Lord, your servant is listening.'" So Samuel went back to bed. And the Lord came and called as before, "Samuel! Samuel!" And Samuel replied, "Speak, your servant is listening" (1 Samuel 3:1-10, NLT).

There are a couple of things the Lord wants to show us in this account with the boy Samuel. He was beginning to hear the voice of the Lord, but what happens? He runs to Eli, the priest—the one who is responsible for hearing from God. The one who is responsible for the *whole nation*. Here is the *one* guy who should be hearing from God, and it takes three times before he finally says, "I think it's the Lord."

Well, let's not be too hard on him; remember what we read at the beginning—messages from the Lord were very rare at that time. He wasn't familiar with the voice of the Lord.

Neither was Samuel at this point, of course, but that's about to change. Notice something interesting—you parents, especially.

When the Lord started talking to this boy, whose voice did it sound like to him?

It sounded like the one who represented God to him—Samuel thought it sounded like Eli's voice. Samuel was serving under Eli, and the priest was teaching him about the Lord—about the Law, about serving the Most High. Samuel's entire life is dedicated to this, since his mom committed him to the Lord after he was weaned. And this man, who is called to instruct him and teach him and show him God's ways, found himself representing God to Samuel.

When Samuel heard God's voice, it sounded like Eli to him.

Parents have such a responsibility—they have so much potential for shaping how their children will hear God. Paul goes back to Abraham as the parent of our faith—of our way of hearing God as believers.

• • •

SAMUEL THOUGHT GOD'S VOICE SOUNDED LIKE ELI'S—THE ONE WHO REPRESENTED GOD TO HIM.

• • •

But there are parents who aren't familiar with the voice of God and don't know how to teach their children to hear Him. For instance, Eli's sons were revolting to God, doing all kinds of evil things; he hadn't taught them to hear God's voice.

So what does it say that so many people think God is angry with them? What does it say that so many think God is looking for excuses to jump on them, to send hurricanes and tornadoes and earthquakes to ruin their day? What does that say about how parents are teaching their children to hear God?

It says we don't know the voice of God.

I've noticed something odd in my own life: there were times,

especially when I was younger, when I was about to sin—
moments before breaking a rule, or split seconds before doing
something I shouldn't—I'd hear my mother's voice. I heard the
voice of the Lord, and it sounded like hers. Because in growing
up in my house, I heard her voice and my father's teaching me
about the Lord. I became familiar with hearing the things of God
through their voices.

So, as a child, when I heard the voice of God, it bore a striking
resemblance to that of my parents.

Take a moment to consider how many people seem to think
God is out to get them, and you can understand why I began with
mercy—we don't understand God because we don't know what
His voice sounds like.

That's why I think it's important that your house begins with
mercy as well. There are standards, and we teach them, but mercy
must be above the rules. Our children must know they can run
to us when they disobey us, because it's vital that they know they
can come to God when they sin against Him.

To Samuel, God's voice sounded like his spiritual father.
Your son or daughter will think God sounds like a spiritual fa-
ther or mother. Will it be your voice that he or she hears when
God speaks?

So Samuel was not yet at a "Hey, it's Me" level with God. He is
hearing God's voice for the first time—at least that we know of.
If God called him on the phone, Samuel would have gone, "Oh,
hey…you. Good to hear from you. Eli? Is that you? I don't recognize this number."

At this point, God needs to say something a few times; it took
Eli and Samuel three times to figure it out. Most of us are at
the same place with God that Samuel was—if that, since many
people don't grow up in the house of God with good spiritual
mentors. For us it may take four or five…or ten times. And
Samuel didn't know to obey right away, perhaps again like you
and me who say, "Well, God's been working on me about that…"

But I want to come to the place when He begins to speak that it's not two, three, four, five times before I catch on that it's God. Don't let it be said of me that the third time I finally say, "I perceive that the Lord is doing something." Let it be the first time.

Now that we've seen Samuel's introduction to God, let's take a look at the process of learning to hear God and recognize it as Him *right away*. The first time...

We Need Help

Something very strange and cool happened to me some time ago. I was preparing for a message, and it seemed right to be speaking on some of these same things we are dealing with now. Only a couple of hours before the service, I felt like the Holy Spirit directed me to some old home videos.

I hadn't looked at these videos in years, and I even had to call my dad to find out if anyone knew where they were. I should have guessed—my dad would know exactly where they were. He pointed me right to them, and without really knowing what I was looking for, I began to watch these old tapes.

The very first one was of me learning to ride my bike. I was probably 5 or 6, and I was learning to ride without training wheels. My dad loaded me in the car, and we headed for an empty parking lot—and the video camera came along.

As I mentioned before, my father might not have been an unrealized pro athlete, but he certainly has a flair for the arts, including theater. So we didn't just record me riding around, we waited for the light to be *just right*. Then my dad recorded me, in my thick, Southern drawl, performing an interview about the feat about to take place.

There I was, holding a microphone in an empty parking lot with the light falling just *so* on my face, dramatically, recording my interview with every one of my five or so years of theater training.

I looked right into the camera, and with zero inhibition said, "Today, this is my second bike ride ever. And sir, would you please show them around?" The camera panned around, then when it came back to me, I bravely said, "This is only my second time to ride by myself. It will be pretty hard, but I can do it without anybody's help."

I can do it without anybody's help.

When I heard myself make that statement, I knew immediately why the Holy Spirit had drawn my attention to this video.

This is a component of every child's life—learning we can do things without anyone's help. Eighteen knots later, we've tied our shoes ourselves. A huge mess in the kitchen, and we've made our own breakfast. After some serious work, we're going to the bathroom by ourselves. And our parents applaud.

•••

THIS IDEA THAT WE CAN DO IT
WITHOUT ANYONE'S HELP HAS NO PLACE
IN OUR RELATIONSHIP WITH GOD.

•••

I remember my little sister learning to go to the bathroom by herself, without anybody's help. It was a huge deal in our house. I was 8 or 9, and I was thinking, *I do that all the time. There's no party when I do this.* Nobody even seemed to care. But when she did it, we picked up the phone. We called grandparents. We called aunts and uncles. We called random phone numbers and told them, "She just went potty all by herself!" But there was no fanfare for me at my age—I already did it on my own.

God used this video to show me something: This concept that we can do it by ourselves, without *anyone's* help, is *best left behind in childhood.* It has no place in our relationship with God.

None.

But all too often, somehow we never quite let go of this desire to be independent. Regardless of what it is, our world is full of adults who say, "I can do this without your help." Including to God. Or, "I'm going to try it myself, and if I need You, I'll come back for help. If I want Your help, I'll ask for it."

But the Lord began impressing on me that this was an immature, childish attitude we really need to lay aside in our relationship with Him. It's interesting that we still do the same thing we did as children of 3 or 4 or 5.

Paul says something interesting about behaving childishly: "When I was a child, I spoke as a child, I understood as a child, I thought as a child; but when I became a man, I put away childish things" (1 Corinthians 13:11). Notice he doesn't say, "I grew out of childish things." He says he put them away.

We grow out of some things. My mom still has boxes of my clothes from when I was 3 and 4 years old. But there is no way I can wear them anymore. Why? Because I have outgrown them. With the exception of a few style-challenged husbands, we grow out of having to be dressed by someone else. Most "grown-ups" don't need to be reminded to brush their teeth before bedtime.

But there are other things we must purpose to put away. I played video games when I was a kid. I don't anymore. I put them away. I used to listen to some pretty heavy music. I don't anymore. I put it away.

•••

HELLO, MY NAME IS
"ALL THE HELP YOU'LL EVER NEED."

•••

There are also mindsets and ways of thinking that are childish. This idea, "I can do it without anybody's help," is one we can put away. For some, "I can ride my bike without anybody's help," somehow turned into, "I can do this relationship without anybody's help." "I can do my job without anybody's help." "I can raise this kid without help."

But when it comes to the things of God, there's no room for this kind of attitude. You can't rely on your own understanding and walk in faith. You'll have to lay this "I can do it without any-one's help" thing aside if you're going to walk in humility before your God.

In reading this book, you're learning to recognize God when you see Him. He has promised to be your ever-present Helper. He is standing there with a name tag on that says, "Hello, My name is 'All the Help You'll Ever Need.'"

But how will you recognize your helper if you don't think you need any help?

Help Me, Jesus!

I want to show you what Jesus said about the help we need. John 14:16-17 says, "And I will pray the Father, and He will give you another Helper, that He may abide with you forever—the Spirit of truth, whom the world cannot receive."

Jesus goes on to say that He taught them as one Man—present in one place at a time. But this Helper would not be limited to be-ing able to teach one sermon at a time: "But the Helper, the Holy Spirit, whom the Father will send in My name, He will teach you all things, and bring to your remembrance all things that I said to you" (verse 26).

In fact, Jesus says something shocking two chapters later. In explaining that He had to leave them, Jesus said, "But because I have said these things to you, sorrow has filled your heart. Never-theless I tell you the truth. It is to your advantage that I go away; for if I do not go away, the Helper will not come to you; but if I depart, I will send Him to you" (John 16:6-7).

Jesus looked at His disciples and said, "You boys need some

help." But the truth is He wasn't just talking to them. He was talking to us, too.

I can imagine how the disciples might have had a hard time processing all of that right away—He was telling them some pretty heavy news. Let's just look back here a moment to see what they'd be losing and put ourselves in their shoes.

Just a few short years ago, Jesus showed up in these guys' lives. Jesus drew disciples from a handful of professions, from tax collectors to fishermen. He had dropped in on their everyday lives and said, "Come, follow Me." And they did—they dropped what they were doing and followed Him. Immediately! From the moment they met Him, their lives were forever changed.

They heard His words, and they responded immediately. And in the next three years, these men—who had probably started their trades because they couldn't make it as some rabbi's disciples—followed around a rabbi who turned water into wine. They watched Jesus open blind eyes. They saw little girls raised from the dead, thousands fed from a little boy's lunch, demons bend their knees in obedience, and the very wind and waves obey Him.

•••

JESUS KNEW WE NEEDED HIM
TO BE EVERYWHERE AT ONCE.
SO HE SENT THE HOLY SPIRIT.

•••

He sent them out in His Name to spread the good news. They came back to Him after seeing Him perform great works through them and were totally stunned. "Even the devils obey us in Your Name!" they told Him. Jesus probably just smiled and nodded.

He had changed their lives forever.

And now He says, "I'm leaving and none of you asks where I am going." I might be standing there saying, "Forget 'where'! I want to know why! *Why* are You about to leave us three short years after changing the rules? Why would You do that, Jesus? Why would You come and change everything and then just leave us alone? I don't want things to go back to the way they were."

And that's when Jesus dropped the bomb: "It's actually for the *best* that I go away."

I'd probably have argued the point. "Uh, Jesus, I remember what it was like before You came along. I was busy fixing nets; I smelled like fish all the time. Life without You was not better. How can it be better for us if You're gone?"

•••

IF JESUS SAID IT WAS BETTER FOR HIM TO GO, THEN THAT IS THE TRUTH. AND IF YOU ARE BEGGING FOR HIM TO SHOW UP, THEN YOUR FAITH IS IN REVERSE.

•••

But Jesus wasn't done. He says, "It's better that I go away, because if I don't, the Helper won't come." He knew they needed help. "Peter," He might have said, "I know you need help. I've heard some of the things you say. You need some serious help."

He knew they needed Him to be *everywhere at once.* He knew we needed the help of the Holy Spirit. The Holy Spirit's help, Jesus implied, was better than the help He provided by being physically in flesh and blood on this planet.

I've heard plenty of people pray as though their lives would be better if Jesus were physically present with them. They seem to ignore this Scripture and the reality that Jesus Himself said it was better that we had the Holy Spirit—the Helper.

Let me encourage you not to pray that way. Don't say things like, "Jesus if You were only here to lay Your hands on me, I know I would be healed." I know it might be tempting to say,

"Jesus, I just need You to show up here and tell me what I am supposed to do."

But if Jesus said it was better for Him to go, then that is the truth. And if you are begging for Him to show up, then your faith is *in reverse.*

He is not unaware of your need for help, just as He was not unaware of Peter's need, and John's need, and Philip's need. He knew they needed help, and He knows we need help, too.

That is why He sent us a tour guide. Let's check His role out together.

Chapter Seventeen

UNLOST

You may recall another scripture we've looked at—John 16:12-13—where Jesus says, "I still have many things to say to you, but you cannot bear them now. However, when He, the Spirit of truth, has come, He will guide you into all truth; for He will not speak on His own authority, but whatever He hears He will speak; and He will tell you things to come."

We looked at this scripture while talking about God's authority, but I feel it's important to remember a key component: This word *guide* Jesus uses in the middle has a very rich meaning. This isn't just saying the Holy Spirit is going to give you a rough outline of how to get where God wants us to go. The connotation here is of a guide who is intimately familiar with the path—every nuance and detail of the route.

Let's say you want to take your family on a weeklong hiking vacation. If you are smart, then you'll hire a guide first thing in order to get your family safely through the mountains. You're hiking for a week, out into territory you don't know, so you bring on someone who does know the area.

The best guide is the one who has lived in this area his whole life. He spent his childhood in these mountains. He knows every campsite. He knows every twist of the trail, every landmark, every river and stream. He knows this country in different seasons, and he even knows the animals that pass through it.

In fact, he's guided so many families, he knows how to pace the hike so you don't get too tired. He knows that the people with him need water and to eat; he knows the dangers posed by the berries by the side of the path or the inviting-looking meadow that has poison ivy lurking in it. He knows the scenic outlooks and where the vistas are the most beautiful and rewarding, and he knows how to get you there by the best route.

How can anyone know so much about every intricate detail of this land? It's simply because he has been there and back, and there and back, and there and back again. He has walked this path so many times, he knows it intimately.

...

WITHOUT THE HOLY SPIRIT AS OUR GUIDE,
WE GET LOST. EVERY TIME.

...

All of that is wrapped up in this word *guide* that Jesus used. And all of this is what Jesus gave us in the Holy Ghost.

But perhaps you're familiar with the father who is more brave than wise. He's the one who says, "No. We don't need a guide. I'm a mountain man myself. I've read all about this mountain. Studied it online."

He thinks he can do it himself, without anyone else's help.

And what happens to this guy, and his family? They get into trouble. They eat the berries, wallow in the poison ivy, and miss out on the beautiful vistas. They get hungry and thirsty because they don't know when to eat or where the cool water is. They have an awful hike; it may even get dangerous.

This is what happens when we try to do without the Helper.

We need help. We need a guide. And that's exactly what the Holy Spirit is—our Helper, our Guide. He's been to where you and I are going. He knows every step—He's been there and back and knows the terrain like the back of His hand. He knows what's around every corner. He knows where the traps are, where the loose rocks are, where the danger lies; and He knows where the most glorious, rewarding views and experiences are.

I learned many of these things from a wonderful man and mentor, Pastor Rick Renner. The statement he made that has stuck with me is that the Holy Ghost knows how to get you there quicker and safer. Thank you, Pastor Rick, for that insight, and thank You, Jesus, for the amazing gift of help You have given Your Church.

Perhaps right now you can better identify with the people who are lost in the woods, so to speak. Without the leadership, direction, and correction of the Holy Spirit, that is exactly what we are—lost. And because our prideful nature isn't always quick to put away this childish "I don't need any help" concept, many believers are lost in the maze of pressing decisions, troublesome relationships, and compromising situations.

Would you like to find out how to get the directions, how to get the information we need, and how to follow it? Want to get unlost?

At the risk of sounding oversimplistic, let's look at three un-complicated components of getting unlost and see if perhaps you may begin to feel differently...

Getting Unlost

Let's take a quick look at Isaiah 55:8-9, which says, "'For My thoughts are not your thoughts, nor are your ways My

ways,' says the Lord. 'For as the heavens are higher than
the earth, so are My ways higher than your ways, and My
thoughts than your thoughts.'"

If you have been in a church service for more than ten minutes, then you have probably heard this scripture. And too many
times, I've heard it used as an excuse—that God is saying, "My
thoughts are not your thoughts and My ways are higher than
your ways, so good luck, pal." But that's not it.

We think, *What's the point in trying? I could never think like
Him. I could never act like Him. His ways are a mystery. Maybe
I'll know when I get to heaven....*

•••

"GOD, I HAVE MESSED THIS THING
UP OVER AND OVER. I'M GOING TO STOP
DOING IT MY WAY AND DO IT YOUR WAY.
I NEED YOUR HELP."

•••

But this verse is not an excuse for copping out or getting
complacent. In fact, misinterpreting this verse is really just a case
study in what happens when we don't look closely enough at the
verse that precedes it (or bother to check it out at all).

Look at verse 7. It says, "Let the wicked forsake his way, and
the unrighteous man his thoughts; let him return to the Lord, and
He will have mercy on him; and to our God, for He will abun-
dantly pardon."

Then God says all that about His ways not being our ways. God
is saying, "My ways are better than yours. So stop doing it your
way and start doing it Mine. My thoughts are higher than yours.
Stop thinking about this the way you were thinking about it, and
start thinking about it the way I do. Return to Me, and leave your
own devices behind."

He wants us to say, "God, I have messed this thing up over and over. I can't figure out how I made such a mess of this. But I'm leaving my ways behind; I'm going to stop doing it my way and do it Your way. I need Your help."

We all know the cliché conversation that's as old as men and women and traveling—I'm sure this conversation went on in covered wagons, just as it does in our cars today.

"We're lost," says the wife. "I know where we are," counters the husband. And then she asks, "Why don't you just pull over and ask for directions?!" And he says, "I don't need to—I don't need directions." He doesn't want to admit he needs help.

But he's lost.

Similarly, we're lost. We've tried it our way, and now we're utterly, totally, and thoroughly lost. So how do we get found again?

Stop

So here is the one, two, three to getting unlost. These may be common sense to some of you, but for others this may be an epiphany. These things are simple, but I guarantee many of us don't do them. For some reason they seem hard.

According to the scripture in Isaiah 55 you read earlier, what's the first thing you do? "Let the wicked forsake his way," it says. So basically, step one is: *STOP.* Simple, right?

But you probably know that this is harder than it seems at first. It's sometimes hard to know *what* to stop or how to halt the momentum of our lives and the events that are spinning

•••

SO HERE IS THE ONE, TWO,
THREE TO GETTING UNLOST:
STOP, ASK, AND FOLLOW.

•••

around out of control. Some of us (Type-A personalities, mostly) feel we're only getting somewhere if we're moving—even if it's the wrong way.

But if you're lost and want to become unlost, the first thing you must do is *stop.*

In a previous section, we took a look at the beginning of Psalm 46: "God is our refuge and strength, a very present help in trouble. Therefore we will not fear," even though all manner of bad things are going on around us. The earth is quaking, the mountains are crumbling, the ocean is roaring and foaming. The nations are in chaos, and they're crumbling, too—perhaps economically.

•••

IN THE MIDDLE OF IT ALL GOD SAYS,
"BE STILL. STOP. I AM STILL GOD."

•••

Despite all this chaos, we receive the word from the Lord in verse 10—the famous verse in this psalm: "Be still, and know that I am God." What do you do? *Stop. Be still.*

Yet while all this craziness is going on, God is not sitting idly by. Remember what I said about reading the preceding verse? You've got to read the verse before this and allow it to paint a picture. In verse 9, God is busy setting up why you should trust Him: "He makes wars cease to the end of the earth; He breaks the bow and cuts the spear in two; He burns the chariot in the fire."

Here's a picture of the earth itself being removed, mountains being thrown into the sea, breaking, and melting. The nations, where we live, are going nuts and crumbling.

And in the middle of it all God says, "Be still. Stop. I am still God."

As I write this, the world economic scene could warrant a description like the one in this psalm. We also see wars, earthquakes, tsunamis—these things are happening in our natural world today. And in the middle of all this, it's our job to be still and hear the voice of the Lord.

But this psalm is also an accurate figurative description of our everyday lives—the craziness, the chaos, the busyness of it all. Even as your schedule crumbles like a mountain falling into the raging sea, you're looking at your checklist and wondering how you'll get the rest of it done. And how often are we looking at those things, and—consciously or not—thinking we can do it all without help? How often do we not even think of turning to Him for help?

You might feel like the world is speeding by you. It makes me think of an interesting special effect I've seen of a guy standing in the middle of a crowded street. Cars are flying past and people are zooming by all around him. But he's just mired there, still. You may feel like that.

In the middle of our crazy lives, our job is the same as it is when the world at large is in chaos: Stop. Be still. Picture yourself as that guy, with the world coursing around him like some frenetic scene from a movie, and know that the peace of God is all over that guy—all over you.

Harder than it sounds?

I get reminded of this on Sunday mornings when I get up to preach. You might think I'd spend the time in prayer, but the first fifteen minutes of consciousness are something like this: *OK, got service today. Then 6 p.m. prayer with the young people. Praying for the West Coast Believers' Convention…got to get some things together for that. Monday: crew meeting before we leave for the convention. Tuesday and Thursday: family functions. Friday, leave for the convention. And don't forget to wash your hair, Jeremy.*

And in the middle of this internal monologue, I feel God impress on me, "Jeremy, stop. Be still." So I calm down for a few moments. But then my mind tends to start up again. *What was it I'm going to say this morning again?*

"No. Stop. Be still. You can't do this without My help." God again. "You need to be still and know that I am God. Stop. Forsake your way. Haven't you figured out yet that this doesn't work for you? Haven't you figured out yet that doing it on your own is not producing anything good? Do you remember what I said…that without Me you can do nothing? So just stop already. Be still."

Perhaps you've tried this—if not, give it a shot. Despite everything there is to think about and to do, you must instead simply *be still*. Take a few moments to try it out. Take a few deep breaths, put all your thoughts and concerns out of your head, and quit reading for a moment. Put the book down.

I bet you picked it right back up, didn't you?

It's surprisingly difficult. And why is that? We feel a need to fill space, to be moving and doing. We have a very, very hard time simply *stopping*. When I preach about this, it's very awkward encouraging everyone to just stop. Standing up there talking about being still, the temptation is to say something (something else that encourages stopping, when in fact I need to be still myself). It's the dreaded awkward silence that we feel obligated to fill up, even if it's with "ums" and "uhs."

•••

DESPITE EVERYTHING THERE IS
TO THINK ABOUT AND TO DO,
YOU MUST INSTEAD SIMPLY BE STILL.

•••

So stopping, being still, is not as easy as it sounds. Yet it's a talent we must cultivate, if we wish to become unlost.

Why? Well, for one reason, recall how the Lord appeared to

Elijah. A windstorm came that even ripped apart the rocks, but He wasn't in the wind. The earth shook, but the Lord wasn't in the earthquake. Then the fire came, but the Lord was not in the fire.

But after the wind and after the earthquake and after the fire, there was a *still, small voice.*

We'd understand God being in the wind, the earthquake, or the fire—an obvious, loud manifestation of His presence that would seem only appropriate for God. Maybe it even seems like it would take God showing up big like that to begin to overshadow the hugeness of our schedules—that He'd overcome our crumbling mountains and roiling seas with the hurricane-force, earthshaking flash-fire of His presence.

•••

TO HEAR A STILL, SMALL VOICE OVER THE CRUMBLING MOUNTAINS AND RAGING SEAS, WE MUST STOP, BE STILL, AND LISTEN.

•••

You'd think He'd just say, "Hello. My name is God." Big and bold as you please.

The wind, earthquake, and fire seem a better match for our lives, a better way for Him to make sure we hear Him. But listening to God in these things wouldn't require any humility. It wouldn't require us shutting our own noise off long enough to pay attention and give Him the place of authority the Most High deserves.

To hear a still, small voice amid the crumbling mountains and raging seas and failing nations, we must stop ourselves and be still. To listen.

If you really experimented with stopping everything a few paragraphs ago or you've tried it before, you know it's hard.

You might say, "I don't have time to stop." But I'd counter with the fact you don't have time *not* to stop.

Decisions must be made. Things must be accomplished. OK, I understand that. But believe me, it'll actually be faster in the long run if you stop first rather than just muddle through.

I find this is frequently true of my own life—many projects I begin never really get rolling, or else meet an untimely death, simply because I made my plans on the run. I didn't stop and really consider it—I should have given it some time and let my thoughts settle before even setting out on my first task. But I didn't stop.

Stopping to think it over is oftentimes the difference between a foolish and wise person. Wisdom stops and prepares, getting itself organized, while everyone else is already running off half-cocked and full steam ahead.

We usually think that no one really has time to *really* prepare these days, perhaps thinking that our ability to multitask has eliminated that need. But, put quite simply, if you don't spend time preparing, you are going to spend time *re*pairing.

Either way, you are spending time at something—so why not spend it on the front end and do it right the first time? That is going to require you to be still for a little while.

As we learned earlier, Jesus knew we would need some help in this. Believe it or not, simply being still is the first step to receiving the help of the Holy Ghost in our lives.

God spoke at the beginning of the universe. God spoke in the Old Testament. God spoke in the time of Jesus. He spoke to the writers of the New Testament.

News flash—He's speaking today. In a still, small voice, He's saying that you must slow down, stop, and be still in order to hear.

That's the first step: If you're lost, stop. The more quickly you do it, the less backtracking you'll have to do to get back on the right path.

Ask

Now that we've got the car pulled over (stopped), what's next? Ask for directions. In a nutshell, that's step two—*ask*. What are we going to ask for?

James 1:5 says something interesting: "If any of you lacks wisdom, let him ask of God, who gives to all liberally and without reproach, and it will be given to him."

I think it's safe to say that sometimes we just don't know what to ask for. We need help to even ask the right questions. Romans 8:26 says, "The Spirit helps us in our weakness. We do not know what we ought to pray for, but the Spirit himself intercedes for us with groans that words cannot express" (NIV).

So you're lost. You stop—be still. Then you fall to your knees and pray, "Holy Ghost, help me! I need wisdom; show me how to pray."

•••

*"IF ANY OF YOU LACKS
WISDOM, LET HIM ASK."*

•••

If we skip this step, we can get all hyped up—the opposite of being still—thinking we're doing the right thing. We pray about this and that, binding these things and loosing those. But which to do first? And which things need binding and which loosing?

We speak to the mountain, as Jesus said, and tell it to move: "Mountain, you be removed and be thrown into the sea." But when we open our eyes, the mountain is still there. *I know what I forgot to do,* we think. *I forgot to say the Name of Jesus.* So we try again: "I speak to you in Jesus' Name."

But the mountain still stands there. It's easy to get yourself worked up this way, losing sleep and wondering why this stuff seems to work for the preacher but not for you.

But when this is happening, you must take a step back. Stop

moving, flailing about, and trying it on your own. Then pull over and ask for directions. Ask for wisdom. God likes to give wisdom, and He will never run you down for not knowing what to do or for being lost. He's not that kind of father.

When we need help, we must ask for it.

I think this is a good place to take a deeper look at the word *help*. When you ask for help, I want you to know exactly what you are asking for according to Scripture. In Romans 8 the word *help* is a Greek word that breaks down into three root words. Now don't skip this, it really is interesting.

The first part of the word bears the connotation of "working together with." This is what the Holy Ghost does on our behalf. This is what the Holy Ghost does with us the moment we stop and ask for help. It's not what He does for us; it's what He does *with* us. The moment we ask for help, there He is alongside us.

It's as if He is saying to you, "All right. Let's get this thing figured out. Let's get you out of this ditch. Let's get you out of this mess. I recognize this mess. You've been here before, haven't you? All right. Let's get you out of this. Let's get you moved on. We're going to get some help for you." And He starts to work together with you.

...

WHEN THE HOLY SPIRIT COMES TO HELP, HE IS ENRAGED AT THE THING THAT HAS YOU BOUND.

...

What's your part in it? Doing what He says. We'll get to that in a second.

The next component of the word gets painted in the Greek with such a vivid picture. It is the word *anti,* and it means "over or against." But that's too mellow a way of saying it. It's used to describe an individual who was so anti-society, so anti-establishment, anti-government, someone who was so against the rules, against everything society stands for that if left unrestrained, this person would do damage.

Does that strike you as a strange description of the Holy Spirit? Well think of it like this: When the Holy Spirit comes alongside you to work with you, He is enraged *at the thing that has you bound.* He is profoundly opposed to anything that sets itself against you—confusion, despair, depression, and oppression. Anything that has tried to set itself against you, He sets Himself against and says, "No. This isn't happening to you. You asked Me for help, and here I come. I'm here to help you, and I'm against this thing with you. We're going to find the answer to this, and we're going to rise above it. We're going to get you out of this ditch. We're going to set you on the path in front of you, and you are going to walk through to victory."

The last part of the word means "to reach out and take."

The moment the answer is in sight, the Holy Ghost Himself— the Helper who has stepped up alongside you—is ready to work together with you, and is so determined to beat this thing that is against you, He reaches out with the arm of faith and pulls that answer to you.

This is the *help* of the Holy Ghost.

Why on earth would I live in this childish concept of "I don't need anybody's help"? This is *who He is.* This is what He does. This is His name!

Hello. My name is God, your Helper.

Some translations of the Bible call Him the Comforter. Some call Him the Counselor, the Standby, the Advocate. If you walked up to a man with a name tag on that says, "Hello. My name is your Helper, Counselor, Standby, Advocate. I'm the one called alongside you," do you think you'd go to him for help? He's the one you'd want to call on.

The Spirit Himself makes intercession for you—comes alongside you to help pull you out of your ditch. He begins to work with you. He begins to work for you. He begins to make your trouble His trouble.

This is the help of the Holy Ghost.

But you've got to stop. You've got to pull over and ask for help from the Helper. Because when you ask, He is right there. And, as we're about to see, His is the voice of Wisdom.

Chapter Eighteen

FOLLOW THE INSTRUCTIONS

The Word paints a picture of Wisdom as a personified individual in Proverbs. It says, "Wisdom shouts in the streets. She cries out in the public square. She calls to the crowds along the main street, to those gathered in front of the city gate" (Proverbs 1:20-21, NLT).

•••

WISDOM CALLS TO US ON THE
STREET CORNERS OF OUR LIVES,
RIGHT WHERE YOU AND I LIVE.

•••

Why do you suppose Wisdom cries out in these particular places? The list doesn't include your prayer closet or church; it doesn't include kneeling by the bed or the study room where you read the Word. I'm not denying that we need to go to these places and do these things, but I was curious what made these others special—streets and public squares and the city gates. What is so special about those places?

Nothing. Nothing is special about them. They just happen to be where you and I live our lives—that's where Wisdom is speaking.

When you're out in the city and you're doing your job, when you're stuck in traffic, when you're driving to the mall or the grocery store, guess who's speaking? Wisdom. The Spirit of God is speaking to you right there.

•••

WHEN WE REJECT WISDOM'S ADVICE,
WE REAP THE FRUIT OF OUR CHOICES.

•••

In this Proverb, Wisdom goes on to ask how long simpletons will insist on being simple-minded. How long will the mockers relish their mocking? How long will fools hate knowledge? I've heard some preachers translate it like this, "Hey stupid! How long are you gonna stay stupid?" (Those are mostly preachers from Texas.)

All the while, Wisdom makes an offer—an alternative to being simple-minded, foolish mockers: "Come and listen to my counsel. I'll share my heart with you and make you wise" (verse 23, NLT).

But there's also a word of warning here—there's a consequence to ignoring the voice of Wisdom. It isn't that Wisdom hunts you down and punishes you; it's that in remaining foolish, simpleton mockers, we get into trouble. When wisdom called, these foolish mockers wouldn't come, and when she reached out, they paid no attention, ignored her advice, and rejected her correction. So it's their own fault when their ways lead to destruction.

And when that day comes, Proverbs says Wisdom will laugh at their trouble and in turn mock them when disaster overtakes them. When the mountains crumble and the storms whip the ocean into a frenzy around them, Wisdom—which could have prevented calamity—will not answer their cry for help or be found despite their searches.

Why? Because they hated knowledge and did not fear the Lord. Because they rejected Wisdom's advice, they're going to reap the fruit of their choices. Their waywardness will lead to their deaths and their complacency will lead to their destruction.

These are some pretty stout words.

Let's make sure they don't apply to us. Don't wait for God to say something three times before you recognize that it's the voice of God, of Wisdom. Don't make Him repeat Himself four or five times before you heed the voice of the Lord, before you stop doing things the way you were.

Proverbs calls this kind of behavior being a simpleton—an idiot. A fool. So let's stop being dumb and go with His higher thoughts, His higher ways. Let's go with Wisdom.

We need to stop and ask for help from the Holy Spirit, our Helper.

Higher

John 16, where we were earlier, tells us what the Holy Ghost, our Helper, speaks to us, not "on His own authority, but whatever He hears He will speak" (verse 13). He's going to tell us God's higher ways and thoughts.

It might look something like this: You're in the middle of trouble such as you've never experienced before; you're facing a giant of a problem. You don't have any idea how you're going to get out. And here comes this higher thought: *You are more than a conqueror through Him who loves you.* Here comes a higher thought: *You can do all things through Christ Jesus who strengthens you.*

You're in a financial crisis that seems like impending ruin. Here comes a higher thought: *You have every single need met that you could ever imagine. All your need is met according to His riches in glory in Christ Jesus.*

You've been diagnosed with cancer. Here's a higher thought: *I've healed you. By My stripes you are healed.*

Your family is one of constant turmoil, and it threatens to spill into your life and pull you down into despair. But here's a higher thought: *When you were born again into Christ, old things passed away. All things have become new. I've adopted you with a Spirit of adoption by which you cry out "Abba, Father."*

These are the higher thoughts, the higher ways. And He begins to communicate to you and me all because we've stopped doing what we were doing and asked for help.

•••

WE MUST SPEAK GOD'S HIGHER THOUGHTS,
NOT JUST THINK THEM.

•••

But these higher thoughts are not supposed to remain only thoughts. They are supposed to turn into words. Second Corinthians 4:13 says, "And since we have the same spirit of faith, according to what is written, 'I believed and therefore I spoke,' we also believe and therefore speak."

I want to show you a trick I learned from my grandfather a long time ago. Silently, I want you to begin counting in your mind from one to ten. Ready? Go. *One, two, three, four, five.* NOW SAY YOUR NAME OUT LOUD. What happened to your counting? It stopped. Even if just for a moment, your thoughts had to give way to your words.

In the same way, thoughts of hopelessness have to give way to words of encouragement. Don't try to fight thoughts with thoughts. You fight thoughts with words. More specifically, you fight them with God's words.

Sarah and I have made the decision that God's Word is the final authority in our lives. It is the first word, the last word, and every word in between. But that doesn't just happen because we want it to.

•••

ITS NOT ENOUGH TO STOP AND ASK FOR HELP; YOU'VE GOT TO FOLLOW DIRECTIONS.

•••

When we read the Bible, we put His Word in our eyes and ears until it becomes what we think about. What we think about produces what we spend our time talking about. Finally, after we have talked about it a lot, we find ourselves actually living what we've been talking about.

And all of this is the result of leaving the old way of thinking and doing things for His higher way.

Follow

All right, so we've halted the momentum, stopped the car, and pulled over. We have even now asked for directions, for help. But there's a third step.

What good are directions if you don't follow them? It would be like our couple on their trip stopping at a gas station, but then the guy gets back in after talking to the attendant and just kind of grunts.

"What did he say?" the wife asks.

"Well, he said if you go down here and turn right, you'll be right there. A quarter mile down on your left. But he doesn't know what he's talking about. I'm going to go back this way and turn left." (There is a word for that, and it is spelled P-R-I-D-E.)

It's not enough to stop and ask for help; you've got to follow the directions you receive. That's step three—*follow instructions.*

Echoing the passage we read in Proverbs, Romans 8:13 says, "For if you live according to the flesh you will die; but if by the Spirit you put to death the deeds of the body, you will live."

We see in the next verse that being led by the Spirit proves something: "For as many as are led by the Spirit of God, these are sons of God" (Romans 8:14). Being led by the Holy Spirit is a defining characteristic of a born-again believer. I want to be the kind of person who is always in the right place at the right time. Not because I'm "lucky," but because I have turned my ear to the Spirit of God in me and let Him tell me where I need to be.

It's not enough to stop and get directions; you must let the Holy Ghost guide you.

The ones who listen to Him, the ones who are correctable, the ones who will stop doing what they were doing, ask for help, and do what He says—these are His sons and daughters in truth. These are the ones He can use. These are the ones He's going to call upon.

We've talked about this idea of being led before—it's that Greek word again that shares a root with our word *agony.* Recognize right here and now that there are times where being led by the Holy Spirit is agony to this flesh—in fact, being led by the Spirit is probably agony to your flesh most of the time, at least at first.

That's why Paul said he crucified his flesh with its passions and lusts; the flesh doesn't like being led anywhere, especially in God's ways instead of its own. He hung it on the Cross, nailed it there, and let God replace it with willingness to heed the voice of His Spirit. He left the weakness of his flesh behind to follow the Spirit of God within him and became willing to obey, willing to do what he was told, willing to pay any price, willing at all costs to be obedient to the voice of the Lord God Himself.

This is only possible with the help of God the Holy Ghost, your

Helper, because we *can't* do it ourselves and without anybody's help. And all of this help is ready and available to you and me if we'll just stop, ask, and follow.

I hope you weren't hoping for more profound, complicated steps to receiving the help of the Holy Spirit, because that's it—stop, ask, and follow. Three simple things every couple lost on a drive needs to learn.

•••

THE HELPER'S JOB IS
BRINGING GRACE, MERCY,
AND PEACE TO OUR LIVES.

•••

Hello. My Name Is God, Your Helper.

You may have noticed how little babies defy the logic of all the rest of creation and cry and cry when they get tired. They don't realize that they'd feel so much better if they'd just go to sleep. Instead, they get worked into a frenzy by crying because they're cranky and easily upset at everyone and everything. It's nobody's fault; they just need a nap.

Now, nobody criticizes a baby for this, but if you or I did this as an adult—just got more and more irritable and cried about it because we didn't know we needed to go to sleep—it would be a different story. We wouldn't get by with pointing the finger at whatever was keeping us awake; we'd be expected to behave like adults and realize that we needed some rest, quit blaming those around us for keeping us up, and go to bed.

But an awful lot of people are crying and crying because they haven't put away the childish notion that they can do everything without anyone's help. They haven't put away this childish behavior that Paul talks about. They are simpletons and fools, and wisdom has no part of their lives; now they are hurting and tired because of the choices they've made.

We say, "I'm a big boy, I can do it *by myself,*" or "I'm a big girl, I don't *need* your help." And we're saying this to God.

Maybe there are some things that you can do, things that you can do and do well. But how much better if you'd open your life to the Helper. Bringing all the grace, mercy, and peace of God to your life, guiding you around the pitfalls and to the best vistas—this is His job. It's who He is and what He does. It's what's written on His name tag:

"Hello. My name is God, your Helper." He's your Standby, your Counselor, your Comforter. And He's really good at what He does.

Getting Directions

We need the help of the Holy Ghost every hour of every day. You probably need help right now as you're reading this book—I needed it to write this. So don't be afraid to come to God in prayer and ask Him for help with all the things for which you need Him. It's not like He doesn't already know.

Wisdom is crying on the streets and crossroads of your life, in the middle of the daily grind that can cause you to think the mountains are crumbling around your ears and the seas are roiling up to flood you. Are your nations overthrown and your seas lashed by gale-force winds? Is your world shaking, the very ground in upheaval all around you?

It's time to take three little steps: *stop, ask, and follow.*

But sometimes how to do these things escapes us. Doing just these simple things can seem complicated, even beyond us. You might think it's easy to say to do these things, and something else entirely to do them. You might think that stopping sounds kind of odd, feel like you're asking the air in front of you for help, and wonder if you'll even be able to interpret any directions you may get.

This is where praying in tongues—praying in the Holy Ghost—comes in. Some people have shied away from this, and some even say that this gift ended with the time of the apostles or that it's inappropriate without an interpretation. I completely disagree; praying in tongues is a vital part of my everyday life.

Don't know what to pray? Don't sweat it—pray in tongues. Remember Romans 8:26: "For we do not know what we should pray for as we ought, but the Spirit Himself makes intercession for us with groanings which cannot be uttered." Some people interpret this scripture as describing speaking in tongues.

•••

DON'T BE AFRAID TO COME TO GOD
IN PRAYER AND ASK HIM FOR HELP WITH
ALL THE THINGS FOR WHICH YOU NEED HIM.
IT'S NOT LIKE HE DOESN'T ALREADY KNOW.

•••

If you have never experienced the infilling of the Holy Spirit with the evidence of speaking in tongues, then my advice to you is wait no longer. I encourage you to read 1 Corinthians 12, 13, and 14. Those chapters are all about the gifts of the Spirit and how they work together with the Love of God in the life of a believer.

This is not a weird thing at all. It is a gift from God Himself, and the Bible tells us that praying this way will strengthen us in our inner man.

But you don't have to take my word for it. Read it yourself. Just say, "Father, I ask You right now to fill me with Your Holy Spirit. I receive Him as a gift from Jesus." Now just begin to pray and praise God, but don't rely on the words you've always used. Let Him fill you with a new sound.

I pray in tongues a lot because I recognize one thing: I need help! I can't do it alone. You want an interpretation of what I'm praying in tongues? Here it is: *I need help! Holy Ghost, help me!* For all I know, that's all I pray. "Lord, I don't want to be a foolish, mocking simpleton; I need wisdom. Help me!"

•••

THE WONDERFUL THING ABOUT
PRAYING IN TONGUES IS THAT
YOU DON'T HAVE TO KNOW WHAT TO SAY.

•••

The wonderful thing about praying in tongues is that *you don't have to know what to say.* That's right—you don't need to have a clue. You can just trust; you can just have faith that the Holy Ghost knows what you need to be praying and is putting it on your lips, bypassing your traitorous flesh.

This is God Himself helping us do what we're called to do, helping us live the way we're called to live. This is the help of the Holy Ghost. Pray in tongues every single day of your life. Call on the help of the Holy Ghost. When you're done praying in tongues, ask Him to tell you what you just said. Ask Him to help you live out whatever it was you just prayed to Him about.

Don't wait until you're neck deep in your roiling ocean and the mountains are already crumbled to dust. God will help you as you call on Him, but there are consequences to being stupid. Life doesn't have a reset button you can just push whenever you like.

•••

WISDOM CALLS OUT ON THE STREET
CORNERS AND AT THE INTERSECTIONS—
IN THE MIDDLE OF YOUR LIFE. ANSWER!

•••

Also, you don't have to wait until you're somewhere special, like in church or your closet. Wisdom calls out on the street corners and at the intersections—in the middle of your life. Answer! Answer while you're stuck in traffic or headed to the grocery store or while you cook dinner. His voice is there. You don't have to be loud and obnoxious about it; pray in the spirit under your breath, just between you and God. In the middle of a world that's falling down around you, God says, "Be still and know that I am God."

So stop. Ask for help, and then fully expect directions.

•••

ASK YOUR HELPER FOR HELP
WITH EVERYTHING YOU DO.

•••

Ask About Everything

You can apply this in every part of your life. It's amazing to me when people realize that they can stop, ask, and follow directions *before* they speak. For many, that is a new concept—one that's foreign to a great many more people. What would happen if we stopped and asked God before we spoke: "Should I say that?"

Often you will find the answer is "No." So follow directions— don't say it.

Stop, ask, and follow. Do it before you make a big decision. Do it before you buy a car or a house. Do it before you go on a date or take a new job. When it becomes second nature, you may find yourself doing it before you do a lot of things. And you might not always hear something; you might not get a veto. But then again, sometimes you will. Sometimes you'll get direction that it's imperative you follow.

This three-step process should be attached to every single thing you and I do in our whole lives. Give the ministry of the Holy Ghost, the Helper Himself, space front and center in every single thing you do. Ask for help in everything you do.

You might think this is going overboard, but I started asking Him about what I should wear in the morning. I know it sounds kind of funny, but what a surprise when one day, I felt like He started working on me about how I dressed to go to work. Now, I wasn't dressed really poorly, nor was I making an effort to cultivate an appearance of excellence. I felt like He was urging me to step it up a little bit—that I'd feel better about myself and look better.

So I've been doing that. I said, "OK. You care what I wear to work? Then You got it."

One morning, when I was in a hurry, I threw on a pair of jeans before work. But just then, I was reminded of what I had heard from Him. I didn't hear some booming voice while I was standing shirtless in my closet. I just heard a gentle witness inside. That's all. No wind. No fire. No earthquake. Just a still small voice that said, "How about some slacks instead?"

So I put the jeans away and grabbed a pair of nicer pants. When I put on the pants, I reached my hand in my pocket and found a folded check. I'm sad to say that it is not unlike me to leave money in my clothes, and while I do need to get better at that, I have to admit it can be a nice surprise in the mornings.

But this was not a check for me. Some time earlier, someone had given me a check made out to our ministry, and I couldn't remember who had given it. And I didn't at all remember what I'd done with that check! In a meeting I was having with my staff, it had come up that no one had seen the check yet, which meant I still had it. But where? I remember asking the Lord to please help me find that check.

Guess what? He did help me. That is who He is. That is what He does.

That check was to help a group of volunteers get to our summer convention, and I don't know if I would have ever found it in time had it not been for the help of the Holy Ghost.

Start with the small things. Get Him involved in these

decisions that seem insignificant to you.

Will God always tell you what to wear? Probably not. Do you stand in front of the closet all day in your undies, waiting for Him to give you a directive about what to put on? Probably not.

But give Him the chance. Stop, ask, and follow. After you've done it a bit, it doesn't take any time at all. You never know; He might just tell you something you really need to know. Wisdom might whisper with a still, small voice in your spirit that you're to do a particular small something that you'd never think of as significant.

You may never know why God might tell you to do something specific or seemingly off-the-wall. You may *never* find out why God had you do something. But perhaps that something impacted a life because you stopped, asked, and followed. Perhaps it'll change your life, or someone else's. Or perhaps you'll just learn to obey, and when He tells you something He won't have to pull out, "Because I said so," to get you to act.

•••

WILL GOD ALWAYS ANSWER YOU
ABOUT EVERY LITTLE THING?
PROBABLY NOT, BUT GIVE HIM A CHANCE.

•••

Stop, ask, and follow regardless. Ask for His help, help from the Helper. I'm telling you, without the grace of the Lord God, I wouldn't know *how* to get dressed. I wouldn't know my own name or be able to take my next breath.

I know I have used some lighthearted examples and that finding money in your pocket doesn't seem like something worth writing about. But the truth is that it only starts there. I know people who were saved from disaster and tragedy because they felt impressed to take the long way to work one day.

I told you earlier about Pastor Rick Renner. He tells a story
that is truly remarkable. He and his wife were in Chicago attending a meeting. Before the evening service, Pastor Rick had the
strangest feeling come over him. He told his wife, Denise, that he
thought the Lord might be telling him to stay in the hotel and not
go to service that night.

"But that doesn't make sense," he said. "Why would we come
here for these meetings but then just sit in the hotel room?" He
went back and forth on this decision until he finally decided that
he was going to go to service. As he and Denise were racing to get
ready, there was a knock on the door, which Rick assumed was
their driver.

•••

To BENEFIT FROM HIS HELP,
WE MUST BE QUICK TO OBEY.

•••

"We'll be down in five minutes," he yelled from inside the room.
When they got downstairs, he noticed that the driver was not
there yet but thought nothing of it. All the way to the meeting
center, Pastor Rick wrestled in his mind whether or not he should
be going. He remained uncomfortable even after arrival. Just
before the meeting started, Pastor Rick turned and told his wife
he had to return to the hotel.

"Stop at the gas station and then the fast-food restaurant. I'm
hungry," Rick told the driver on their way back to the hotel.
When he finally arrived back at his room, he walked in, utterly
shocked to find that someone had broken in and stolen everything of value in their room. His computer with decades of
preaching notes and manuscripts for books—gone. All of
Denise's jewelry—gone.

They pastor a church in Moscow and were only visiting the
U.S., so you can imagine how his heart must have sunk when he

realized their passports were gone too. When he put it all together, he realized it was not the driver knocking at his door. It
was the thief. Someone had been watching them all week and had
their schedule timed perfectly. And Pastor Rick had told the thief
they would be leaving in five minutes!

What a hard lesson! What if he had obeyed? Instead of attending the meeting, what might have happened had he sat in his hotel
room that night as the Lord had led?

The answer is "nothing." Nothing would have happened. He
might have sat there all night and gone to bed, curious as to
why. But it is far better to trust the Lord and be curious than to
have everything stolen because you chose not to listen. When He
speaks, we must listen.

I know my life has been saved because of obedience to the
leading of the Holy Spirit. There may come a time that you sit at
home bored on a Friday night because the Spirit of God checked
you about going out that night. But would you rather be bored at
home or sitting in a hospital room? You may think that sounds
a little dramatic, but I am only telling you what I have seen and
experienced. We must trust that the leadership of the Holy Spirit
is rooted in God's love for us; and if He loves us, then His direction is always for the betterment of our lives.

Being saved is more than a prayer that you prayed one day.
Salvation is for every day of our lives. He saved you from hell in
eternity, and He is saving you from hell on earth.

If you'll let Him.

God cares about everything in our lives and has made help
available. But to benefit from this help, we must be quick to obey.

The Path of the Righteous

He is God your Helper, and He is faithful to help and guide you every step, every moment. But when we think we know better and choose to take the way that seems right to us, we are literally taking our lives into our own hands.

The psalmist says that there is a way that seems right to a man but that it ends in death. But the good news is found in Proverbs 4:18, which says, "But the path of the [uncompromisingly] just and righteous is like the light of dawn, that shines more and more (brighter and clearer) until [it reaches its full strength and glory...]" (AMP).

That's the path your Guide sets before you. With the help of the Holy Ghost, the steps that we are supposed to take are getting brighter and brighter all the time. There doesn't have to be confusion. There doesn't have to be doubt. There is no darkness on the path that we are on. The help of the Holy Ghost puts us on the right path.

So be willing to stop, ask Him for directions, and follow them.

SECTION VII

JESUS IS

Chapter Nineteen

THROUGH HIM, FOR HIM

We began by discussing the goodness and mercy of God, which became real to me as I studied on this attribute of God's personality. I hope by reading that section you began to fully grasp exactly what kind of God we serve—and that His mercy really does endure forever.

Similarly, we looked at God's authority as well as our own lack of ability to get anything done on our own, which I think of, affectionately, as the kick in the pants that we all need. Keith Moore, of Faith Life Church in Branson, Missouri, taught an outstanding series on this that changed my life and thinking and provided a lot of the impetus for section three.

I pray you saw that leaning on your own understanding won't cut it—it can't, because you can only rely on where you've been, and trusting God takes you into uncharted waters.

But then we also looked at Jesus' presentation of His Father's attributes and at God as a Father—a Father whose interaction with His children is predicated upon our understanding that He is good and merciful and is in complete authority. We saw how in giving us an example of true faith, Paul had to go all the way back to Abraham, the spiritual father of our own faith. Abraham set such an example of trusting God that he was even willing to sacrifice the child of promise, Isaac, to God—fully expecting God to be faithful anyway.

Hopefully, you walked away understanding how we must shape our lives to fit God's Word, not the other way around.

And with the understanding that God is good and merciful, that He is in authority, and that He's our loving Father, we also got to know God as our Healer. We saw that we must believe that He *is,* and that He's a rewarder of those who seek Him—these things are prerequisites for the kind of faith that gets God's attention, as Jairus and the woman with the issue of blood got Jesus' attention.

I'd like to think that after reading that, you'd understand what's involved in seeking God for the answer to your own needs, just as these people trusted that Jesus was the answer to their own needs for healing. This kind of thinking isn't manipulation; it's simply learning how it works, and then purposing to be the kind of person who has the kind of faith that makes Jesus stop and take notice.

And after considering Jesus as our source of healing and the Holy Spirit as our Guide, I'd like to finish our study of the character of God on a final, transcendent note. This God in whom we believe—who exists as described in the Bible as the only One who is good and merciful, as the One who is in authority, as our Father, as our Healer, and as our Guide—is far more than any of these things, yet so simple we can summarize Him with one name.

So let us end with the summation of all He is by discussing the One who lives within us when we open our lives to Him and accept salvation. We end with the One who existed from the beginning, the Alpha and Omega.

We end with Jesus.

Jesus Is

Together as a body, our church reads a chapter a day of the New Testament. I can't say enough about how wonderful this practice is, how it brings us together around the Word and forms a corporate backbone and singular purpose throughout our church body.

We came to a time on the calendar when we were to read together the book of Acts. I've read Acts before, but this time something new started looking me in the face. It's particularly evident in the life and ministry of Paul and the other apostles. One passage soon after Paul's conversion on the Damascus road reads, "But Saul increased all the more in strength, and confounded the Jews who dwelt in Damascus, proving that this *Jesus is* the Christ" (Acts 9:22).

•••

EVERYTHING WE NEED, JESUS IS.

•••

Later, in chapter 10, Peter reaffirms the mandate the Lord gave them: "And he [Jesus] ordered us to preach everywhere and to testify that *Jesus is* the one appointed by God to be the judge of all—the living and the dead" (verse 42, NLT). He's the Messiah.

The Holy Spirit compels Paul to preach that *Jesus is* the Messiah in chapter 10—it's what he preached wherever he went. We read this again and again in Acts.

Jesus is the Christ, the Messiah, the Redeemer. *Jesus is* the Word fulfilled. *Jesus is* prophecy made flesh. The New Testament is full of this singular testimony: *Jesus is.*

In Romans 10, it says that if we confess with our mouths that *Jesus is* the Lord and believe in our hearts that God raised Him from the dead, we'll be saved. In 1 John 4 it says that those who confess that *Jesus is* the Son of God, are of God. First John 5 tells us that those who overcome the world are those who believe that *Jesus is* the Son of God.

I could go on and on like that, because the Word is full of affirmations that *everything we need,* **Jesus is.**

The Visible Image of the Invisible

We rightly hear a lot about being more like Jesus, but this book is about learning God's personality. And there is no single way of describing God that is better than the total summation of Himself He put on display on this earth: His Son, Jesus.

This Jesus, Paul tells us, "is the visible image of the invisible God" (Colossians 1:15, NLT).

Paul is explaining to them why we're thankful to the Father. He explains that God qualified us who were sinners to be partakers of an inheritance shared with His people, the saints of the light, and that He has delivered us from the power of darkness and conveyed us into the kingdom of the Son of His love (Jesus again).

Paul explains that in Jesus we are having redemption—present tense. Not we *were* redeemed; we *are being* redeemed. Today. Now. Redemption is something that began on the Cross, was completed through the resurrection, and is taking place *right now.*

He goes on to give us arguably the best summation in all of Scripture about who Jesus is by telling us that He is "the firstborn over all creation." God's Son. "For by Him all things were created that are in heaven and that are on earth, visible and invisible, whether thrones or dominions or principalities or powers." He's the vehicle, the author, of Creation. "All things were created through Him and for Him." He made it all. "He is before all things, and in Him all things consist." He existed before anything else, and He holds it all together. "And He is the head of the body, the church," He's our leader, our Husband. And He is "the beginning, the firstborn from the dead, that in all things He may have the preeminence" (verses 15-18).

These are the best four verses on the character of Jesus, perhaps anywhere. He's the Son of God, but the Spirit of God inspiring this scripture is not satisfied to leave it at that.

Who is God's firstborn Son? Jesus is.

Who is the Creator of *all* things? Jesus is.

Who was before all things and the One in whom all things hold together? Jesus is.

Who is the Head of the Church? Jesus is.

Who is the first One born from the dead? Jesus is.

Who is first in everything, preeminent? Jesus is.

Notice the two realms that He is Creator and Lord over—the visible and the invisible. Try to think of something that does *not* fall into one of those two categories. If you can come up with something that doesn't cover, you're doing better than I. But until we think of something that doesn't qualify as visible or invisible, we can confidently say that He's Lord over it all.

How is this possible? How can all of this—all of the wonder and power of Creation, all of the glory and eminence of God Himself—be revealed in the skin of the human being that Jesus became when He took on flesh?

Paul explains: "For God in all his fullness was pleased to live in Christ, and through him God reconciled everything to himself. He made peace with everything in heaven and on earth by means of Christ's blood on the cross" (verses 19-20, NLT).

He has reconciled all things on earth. Are you a thing on earth? I'm a thing on earth. He's reconciled us. How did He reconcile us? Through the blood of His Cross.

Which ones of us? All of us who were far away from God and who were once His enemies—which includes all of us, period—because of our sins of thought and action.

But He reconciled us to Himself because Jesus took our sins on His physical body, thus bringing us into God's presence holy and blameless.

Come Together Around Jesus

We should be talking about Jesus all the time. In a day when the Body of Christ seems to be arguing with itself more than ever, it seems to me we can all find common ground in the person and power of Jesus Christ.

Personally, I believe that miracles still take place today. I believe that God is the Healer and not the oppressor. I believe that speaking in tongues is a gift that is for everyone in the Body of Christ. I believe that God wants His people to be blessed in every area of life.

•••

> IT SEEMS THAT WE SPEND A GREAT DEAL OF TIME TALKING ABOUT WHAT WE DON'T BELIEVE, RATHER THAN AFFIRMING WHAT WE DO BELIEVE BASED ON THE WORD OF GOD.

•••

Now, you and I may not agree on every one of those, but that's OK. I heard a man say once that we can disagree without being disagreeable. To me, that means even if we don't see eye to eye on everything, we can still come together around our common conviction that Jesus IS the Son of the living God. We can work together in the kingdom of God because we believe that Jesus IS the way, the truth, and the life.

Do you want to see people born again into the family of God? So do I. I believe Jesus IS. And if you do too, then you and I are members of the same family, and I pray that is enough to keep us free from strife and confusion.

Let's put the bickering aside and come back to the common ground of Jesus Christ. It seems that we spend a great deal of time talking about what we *don't* believe, rather than affirming what we *do* believe based on the Word of God.

•••

THE ENTIRE BIBLE
POINTS DIRECTLY AT JESUS.

•••

Him We Preach

If you are a preacher reading this book, I want to encourage you with something out of this same chapter in Colossians. Verses 27-28 have become the foundation for my life and ministry:

> To them God willed to make known what are the riches of the glory of this mystery among the Gentiles: which is Christ in you, the hope of glory. Him we preach, warning every man and teaching every man in all wisdom, that we may present every man perfect in Christ Jesus.

Notice he says that it is God's will for you and me to become acquainted with this mystery: "Christ in you, the hope of glory." What a life-altering reality! Christ, the Anointed One and His Anointing, is living in you!

The three words that follow this statement have changed my motivation in ministry forever: "Him we preach." Did you hear that, preachers? The subject and content of every sermon for the rest of our lives should be as follows: Jesus.

If that sounds limited to you, then may I humbly suggest that you don't know Him well enough? The entire Bible points directly at Jesus. You can find Him all the way through. I challenge you to study the Word from this perspective. The Word reveals Him as God in the flesh—the express image of God our Father.

Jesus Himself said that if you have seen Him, you have seen the Father. Preach Jesus.

The Word Made Flesh

There are countless things we could say Jesus is. We could easily have filled this book talking about Jesus, but let's take this section to bring everything we've learned about God into focus by focusing on Jesus.

John 1 gives us the first thing I want to say about Jesus: *Jesus is the Word made flesh.*

In John 1:1-2 we find that "In the beginning was the Word, and the Word was with God, and the Word was God. He was in the beginning with God." It goes on to say, "All things were made through Him, and without Him nothing was made that was made." Sounds a lot like Colossians. "In Him was life, and the life was the light of men. And the light shines in the darkness, and the darkness did not comprehend it." Skip down to verse 14: "And the Word [Jesus] became flesh and dwelt among us, and we beheld His glory, the glory as of the only begotten of the Father, full of grace and truth."

The Word became flesh. He took on physical aspects down here, where we could see Him—the visible image of the invisible God. Until Jesus came, people could not see God when they worshiped Him. But then Jesus came, becoming tangible, touchable, viewable flesh, and Him they could see.

The writers of the New Testament were men who either saw or were influenced by those who watched Jesus perform miracles. They wrote their testimonies about the Person they saw—the

Word made flesh—walking around on this earth, right in front of their eyes, demonstrating the Father to them.

Their eyes beheld the Word performing miracles and showing them the Father. In one passage, we read that they handled the very Word of God—they lived in such close proximity, they brushed shoulders with the Word given flesh.

You want to know what God looks like? Look at Jesus. He is the image of the invisible God.

You want to know what God sounds like? Listen to Jesus. He spoke nothing on His own, but only what the Father bade Him say.

You want to know what God acts like? Watch Jesus. He did the Father's will on earth.

•••

HE IS THE WORD, AND WHEN JESUS IS THE TEACHER AND THE HOLY SPIRIT IS YOUR GUIDE, YOU LEARN AND GROW FROM WHAT YOU HEAR.

•••

When you read the New Testament—especially what the Spirit of God said through Paul, and the books of Hebrews and Revelation—you begin to see this place of pre-eminence we read about in Colossians. Jesus is the Word made flesh, so His pre-eminence means that He has the first word, the last word (the Alpha and Omega), and every word in between.

Teacher, Preacher, and Healer

From the Gospel account of His life, we learn that everywhere Jesus went, He taught in their synagogues, preached the good news of the gospel, and healed all those who were sick and oppressed by the devil.

He was a teacher, a preacher, and a healer.

When Jesus taught the Word, you didn't leave complaining that He wasn't a good teacher. He *is* the Word, and when Jesus is the teacher and the Holy Spirit is your guide, you learn and grow from what you hear.

He was sent to bring light, and when Jesus is the teacher, you walk in the light. When Jesus is the preacher, you're not bored. When Jesus is the preacher, you don't say, "Oh, this one again?" When Jesus is the preacher, you don't pick and choose which Sundays you come to church. You're there every time the doors are open.

Some of you may read that and think, "Well, yeah, all those people had Jesus in the flesh. If I had Jesus in the flesh, I'd feel the same way."

But remember, Jesus looked His disciples in the eye and said it was better for them if He *wasn't* there. Because if He went, He'd send the Helper. And the Helper, you'll remember, also doesn't speak on His own—He reveals to us what the Father and the Son tell Him.

You may not have Jesus here in the flesh today, but you have His Word and His Spirit. And with that, you have the ability to see plainly the character and nature of God.

So when you listen to the Holy Spirit, you're listening to Jesus. When you learn to receive from the Holy Spirit, you're learning to listen to the very voice of God the Father and His Son Jesus Christ.

When you read the Word, you're hearing from Jesus. You're reading about God's attributes, character, thoughts, and ways. You're reading about Jesus, the visible image of God sent to change the course of history and change all the rules.

So if Jesus is the Word of God, what you hear from the Bible is what you're hearing from God. Jesus is the voice of God, and when you hear the voice of the Holy Spirit, guess who you're hearing—Jesus. That's direction from the throne of God.

Do you think maybe we should take it a little more seriously than we have? Do you think learning to hear the voice of the Holy Ghost may just be one of the most important things you'll ever do?

When Jesus is your teacher, you get it. When Jesus is your preacher, you get excited. When Jesus is the preacher, you listen. It stirs in you, and you get excited because *He knows the Word.* And He's showing it to you, revealing it to your spirit.

Because He's the Word made flesh. After all, He's the first in line. He's the beginning and the end. He has pre-eminence. This preacher is the image of the invisible God.

He's still doing it. He's still the Word, and He looks back at you every time you look at Him in the Bible.

And it changes you. You become what you look at—the Word made flesh, Jesus Christ.

So Jesus is the Word made flesh.

Chapter Twenty

To: You   From: God

In addition to the fact He is the Word made flesh, the second thing I want to say about who Jesus is is that He is the fulfillment of Bible prophecy. Jesus is the fulfillment of well over three hundred Old Testament prophecies, not the least of which was this one: "Surely he took up our infirmities and carried our sorrows, yet we considered him stricken by God, smitten by him, and afflicted" (Isaiah 53:4, NIV).

Isaiah 53:5 offers even more proof that Jesus is the Word made flesh: "But He was wounded for our transgressions, He was bruised for our iniquities; the chastisement for our peace was upon Him, and by His stripes we are healed." This Word of God to and through the prophet Isaiah became flesh when Jesus endured the cross. More than seven hundred years before Jesus ever showed up, the prophet Isaiah was saying, "By his stripes we are healed."

Throughout the Old Testament, from Genesis on, we read this subtext: He's coming, He's coming, He's coming. He's promised to crush the serpent's head, in Genesis.

And all of history was pointing to that moment when the Word became flesh and Jesus fulfilled prophecy, including being your healer. All of history was moving toward a point on the calendar that hadn't even been yet—it didn't yet exist, but it was promised, and godly men and women looked for it earnestly.

The Word became flesh, dwelled among us, and went to the Cross, where He died for our sins. Then rose from the dead with the keys of death, hell, and the grave. All of prophecy, all of God's plan for each of us for eternity, hung on that moment. The Word became flesh, and He fulfilled every one of God's promises regarding the Messiah.

Jesus came and fulfilled the prophecy that His wounds would heal us. If Jesus is your healer, you walk away healed. If Jesus is your healer, you walk away whole.

•••

WHEN YOU HEAR, FAITH COMES.

•••

We've already looked at some examples in this book of Jesus' healing at work, and I've shared some of my favorites—Jairus and the woman with the issue of blood being chief among them. Jairus' daughter was sick to the point of death—actually did die—and the woman had been sick for years and years. But they sought Jesus out with their needs, and He met them. They both got what they came for.

People who need healing can get discouraged, but we see that Jesus, the visible image of the invisible God, healed those who came to Him. That's inspiring to me. People wonder if it's God's will to heal them, but when these people and countless others came to Him, they got what they came for because He is the healer. The Gospels are full of account after account of His willingness to heal—again and again it says He healed them *all*. He had compassion on them, and He healed them.

And these people didn't have the New Testament to quote. They hadn't read Paul's writings, or John's, or Peter's. They weren't walking around quoting 1 Peter 2:24, that by His stripes we're healed. They didn't know there was a 1 Peter, let alone a second. *Why so many Peters?* they would've asked. The woman with the issue of blood was not confessing 1 Peter. There was no such thing yet.

In fact, most of them probably hadn't connected the prophecies regarding the Messiah with this Man, Jesus, yet. "By his stripes we were healed" was nothing more than an unfulfilled prophecy at that point. He was in the process of revealing Himself as the fulfillment of this prophecy.

Yet, the moment that woman with the issue of blood reached out and touched the edge of His garment, she became a part of the fulfillment of the prophecy found in Malachi 4:2, "But to you who fear My name The Sun of Righteousness shall arise with healing in His wings." Interestingly, the edges of the kind of garment Jesus was wearing were commonly referred to as "wings." Whether she knew it or not, there was healing power in the wings of that garment just as Malachi said there would be.

They came believing in Him. They'd heard about Him, and faith arose. When you hear, faith comes. So they sought Him out—did whatever they had to do, offended whomever they had to offend, and disregarded everything but getting to Jesus. All they knew was Jesus.

They knew He'd done it for others, and He could do it for them—not because they'd read the revealed words of men who had connected the prophecies with the One who fulfilled them, but because they heard of and believed in Him.

Jesus Is: Your Gift From God

You may be familiar with a little scripture from John 3:16: "For God so loved the world" that He did what? "He gave His only begotten Son." God gave Him. Jesus is our gift from God.

Romans 8:31-32 says, "If God is for us, who can ever be against us? Since he did not spare even his own Son but gave him up for us all, won't he also give us everything else?" (NLT).

If He gave you the very best, if He started by giving you the very best, is there something better than Jesus that you didn't get? No—He's pre-eminent, first in line. And God *started* with that.

So if He gave you Jesus, would He spare healing from you? No! Jesus *is* your healing, the prophesied healer of your body who took stripes on His back for your healing.

If He gave you Jesus, would He keep peace from your heart and mind? No. Jesus is the Prince of Peace.

If He gave you Jesus, would He keep your marriage from being healthy and whole? Of course not. He's the One who binds a man and woman together as one.

If He gave you Jesus, would He withhold a financial blessing or breakthrough in your life? No. Our God supplies all our need according to His riches in glory...by *Christ Jesus!* He is your supply!

When He gave you Jesus, He gave you His name, His blood, His power, His faith, His ability, and His love and compassion. All of this belongs to you because Jesus belongs to you, and you belong to Him.

•••

BETTER YET, GET GOD INVOLVED
BEFORE TROUBLE COMES.

•••

Jesus told His disciples that they could ask the Father anything *in His name,* and it would be done for them. That is a marvelous promise! He said ask and it will be given to you. Seek and you will find.

I think people have a concept that God is the one hiding things from them and withholding from them so they will learn a lesson. Listen, God is not cruel. Remember, there are things that are a mystery, but they are mysteries hidden *for* us not *from* us.

We just read from Colossians that He willed to make known the mystery: Christ in you the hope of glory. Did you catch it? That is His will. His will is not to keep you in the dark just so He can break you down emotionally so that all that's left to do is cry out to Him.

...

THE LIFE OF A MAN OR WOMAN OF FAITH
IS NOT A LIFE FREE FROM TROUBLE.
THE DIFFERENCE IS, AS A PERSON OF FAITH,
YOU KNOW WHAT TO DO WHEN TROUBLE COMES.

...

If you have not called on God and you are distraught mentally, emotionally, or physically, that is not God's fault. His Word has always been there, and He has not changed. He would have brought you from darkness to light if you had called on Him the moment trouble showed up.

Or, better yet, got God involved *before* trouble came.

The life of a man or woman of faith is not a life free from trouble. The difference is, as a person of faith, you know what to do when trouble comes. What a comforting thought to know that the answer is already within you! How do you know that? Because Jesus is within you, and He is the answer to every question, trial, and problem. When God gave you Jesus, He gave you *the* Answer.

If He gave you Jesus, He'll give you anything else. That's what the Word says.

Jesus is your gift from God.

Jesus Is: All You Need

Second Corinthians 8:9 says, "For you know the grace of our Lord Jesus Christ, that though He was rich, yet for your sakes He became poor, that you through His poverty might become rich." Jesus is the measure of your wealth.

Your effort is not the measure of your wealth. Neither is your position and standing, or who you know. Your bank account and stock holdings are not the measure of your wealth.

Only Jesus is the measure of your wealth.

The wealth of healing that is inside of you, the wealth of peace, the wealth of wisdom, the wealth of grace, the wealth of prosperity and blessing that's promised in the Word of God—these are all in Jesus. It would be good to be rich in those things, wouldn't it? He is the measure of your wealth.

So how are your needs met? I am a firm believer in the biblical concept of having the right confession. Proverbs says that life and death is in the power of the tongue.

Let me explain what I mean. As a fourth-grader at a Christian school in Fort Worth, Texas, I once conducted a science experiment to see how our words can affect the world around us.

I took two identical plants and began to talk to them. "Talk to them?" you ask. Yes. Talk to them. I gave them both the same amount of water, sunlight, and food. The only difference was *how* I talked to them. I told one plant that it was strong, and beautiful, and healthy. I told the other one that it was weak and dying. I did this for weeks.

For a while, nothing seemed to be happening. Both plants seemed to be maintaining similar results. Discouraged—and a little nervous about what kind of grade I might get on a failed experiment—I went to my mom and complained that it wasn't working.

"Yes, it is," she said.

"No, it's not. Look!" I replied.

"Jeremy," she said, "it is working."

A little frustrated by her inability to accurately observe what was going on, I argued and argued with her. Over and over again, I complained that this confession thing wasn't working.

And over and over she calmly replied, "Yes, it is."

Then, all at once, like someone had flipped the switch, it dawned on me: She had the right confession. The whole experiment was based on the power of our words, and there I stood proclaiming (crying, as my mom remembers it), "It's not working! It's not working!"

Right then I realized that it wasn't about what we could see on the outside. It was about the effect that my words were having whether I could *see* it or not.

My experiment concluded with remarkable results: Two plants that received the same light and water came out looking totally different *because of the words I spoke over them.* One was healthy and strong, the other dying and wilting. It was astounding.

But the truly amazing part of this story came long after the science project was over. My mom decided to keep the plants as houseplants, but soon her good intentions turned to neglect and they got stuffed behind a shelf without water or light.

•••

IT IS VITALLY IMPORTANT THAT
WHAT WE SAY ABOUT OURSELVES
IS WHAT THE BIBLE HAS SAID ABOUT US.

•••

Months later, she found them and was shocked by what she saw. The plant that I had been nice to was still alive! The other one had died, and, apparently, it had been dead for some time. But the life-giving power in my words had kept the other little plant alive without light or water for who knows how long!

I tell you this story for a couple of reasons. One, you must be watchful over the words that come out of your mouth about yourself and others. Be watchful over what you say to and about your children. You have the ability to build up or destroy simply by the words you choose.

•••

OUR WORDS REVEAL OUR HEARTS.

•••

It is vitally important that what we say about ourselves is what the Bible has said about us.

But secondly, once you realize that there is indeed power in your confession, you must not be tempted to put your faith in your confession. Your confession is nothing more than a demonstration of your faith, of what and in whom you believe.

I have had the privilege of growing up in a ministry and family that has taught extensively on confession and have, as a result, seen astounding results. But I have also been around long enough to watch as people "try" the confession thing for a while and then walk away discouraged and mad because it didn't work for them.

This isn't something you *try*. This is a way of life. Our words reveal our hearts.

I have also watched people take this revelation and then separate it from the Revealer. What do I mean by that? If you're just confessing "My needs are met" all day, but you're looking at bills that are due and empty bank accounts, are your needs met? No. But when you complete that confession saying, "My God shall supply all my need according to His riches in glory by *Christ Jesus,*" you're recognizing that Jesus is the measure of your wealth (Philippians 4:19).

"My needs are met" is a positive affirmation, but it lacks the life-giving power that comes when you realize that your needs are met *through and by Jesus Christ.* When your confession comes out of what you believe about Jesus to be true, there's power in it. Enough power to change the very circumstances around you. Enough power to renew your mind to a new way of thinking— God's way of thinking.

But you can't confess that and believe it as long as you still view some man or woman, job, or winning lottery ticket as your source. God is your one and only source. He is the measure of your wealth.

We must realize that there are many channels, but only one source. That job you have may be a gift from God. But don't limit Him by viewing that paycheck as your sole means in this life.

Turn that paycheck into seed. He said that He would provide seed to the sower. "Thank You, Lord, for the seed You have brought into my life. Where would You have me sow it?" The simple act of tithing and giving can open the windows of heaven above you, and God has promised to pour out a blessing so big that it will begin to overflow your life.

"Jeremy, you sound like one of those 'prosperity preachers,'" you might be saying.

Well, if by "prosperity preacher" you mean, "Beloved, I pray that you may prosper in all things and be in health, just as your soul prospers" (3 John 1), then, yeah, I guess I am.

But let me tell you what I believe is *true* prosperity.

My wife and I recently committed to what we called "Thirty Days of Giving." This isn't something our church or friends were doing. It is simply something the Lord put on our hearts, so we did it. We committed that we would tithe and sow as normal into our church and other ministries, but in addition to that we looked for an opportunity to give no matter how large or small every day. We have missed a couple days, but mostly we have held to our commitment.

Some days we bought someone's coffee, lunch, or dinner. One day we bought a gift card for our neighbors, who are expecting their third child. Other days, the Lord led us to give hundreds at a time to a friend or family member.

We've had it in our hearts for some time now to give our car away, and the Lord put that in our hearts again in those thirty days. But instead of running out and giving it to the first person we saw, we spent time and money fixing that car and getting it into the best condition possible before we gave it away. That excites us!

"But, Jeremy, aren't you afraid that it might be difficult with only one car? What if you don't get another one for a long time?"

No! I am not afraid! Why? Because Jesus is the measure of my wealth!

I already have proof that what I am saying is true. As soon as we made this commitment to give, the money started coming in to us! I gave away a suit, and a couple of days later someone gave me three shirts and a tie. We told our cousins that we would buy their ski-lift tickets on vacation; the next day my dad told us he would be buying ours. This kind of thing has happened over and over.

•••

THE MEASURE OF YOUR STRENGTH IS IN JESUS.
THE MEASURE OF YOUR ABILITY IS IN HIS ABILITY.

•••

We have had more unusual and extraordinary expenses in these thirty days than we have ever had. And yet, at the end of the day, there is plenty left over. How could that be? It is because Jesus is the measure of our wealth. We are blessed to be a blessing. It thrills us to no end to give to others, because we know it thrills God to give to us.

And try as we may, we just can't seem to out-give Him. No, we are not giving to get. However, you cannot get around the fact that this is God's established system of increase.

In the world's system, if you want to have more, then you had better keep every last nickel you can get your hands on. But when God is your source, if you want to increase, then you had better start looking for a place to give!

When we get into tough financial situations, the first thing we do is look for a place to sow. That's just the way it is for us. That is the prosperity message we preach and the one we live.

Jesus is the measure of our wealth.

Not only is He the measure of your wealth, He's also the measure of your strength. Philippians 4:13 says, "I can do all things through Christ who strengthens me." *The Amplified Bible* expands on this: "I have strength for all things in Christ Who empowers me [I am ready for anything and equal to anything through Him Who infuses inner strength into me; I am self-sufficient in Christ's sufficiency]."

What you've been through and what you've accomplished isn't the measure of your strength. What you've overcome is not the measure of your strength. Your determination, discipline, and character are not the measures of your strength.

The measure of your strength is Jesus. The measure of your ability is in His ability. Your only self-sufficiency is in Christ's sufficiency. You have conquered some things, but only because He has conquered *all* things.

The Measure of Your Ability

Jesus is also the measure of your ability. John 15:5 says, "I am the vine, you are the branches. He who abides in Me, and I in him, bears much fruit; for without Me you can do nothing." But with Him, all things are possible.

Recall our "In You" truths—without Him you are nothing, know nothing, have nothing, and can do nothing? That's because Jesus is the measure of your ability. We've got to remind ourselves of this: Without Him, we can do nothing.

We must be especially careful of this after we've seen and done some things; after we've been around the block a few times, we

can start leaning on our own understanding. We can start looking at what we've lived through, what we've seen, and what we've
experienced. And we can think that qualifies us or that enables us
to do it without anyone's help.

If you've been through some stuff, the Lord has indeed taught
you, but you're only capable through Him. Your ability is in Him,
not in yourself. We must all learn this early on and keep learning it again and again. It is not about what we can do in and of
ourselves, but what we do through Him.

Remember Proverbs 3:5-6: "Trust in the Lord with all your
heart, and lean not on your own understanding; In all your ways
acknowledge Him, and He shall direct your paths."

Let's revisit this as well—according to that scripture,
the opposite of trusting the Lord is leaning on your own
understanding. You cannot get more opposite; you cannot
get more diametrically opposed to trusting in God than
leaning on your own understanding.

Trusting in yourself will only get you as far as you've ever been.
At the very best, it may get you as far as somebody else has been.
But trust in Him will take you places nobody has been. Trusting
Him as the measure of your wealth, your strength, and your abil-
ity lets Him take you where He desires you to go.

Chapter Twenty-One

YOU'RE WORTH IT

Jesus is the Word made flesh. Jesus is the fulfillment of prophecy. Jesus is your teacher, preacher, and healer. Jesus is your gift from God. Jesus is the measure of your wealth. Jesus is the measure of your strength. Jesus is the measure of your ability. And lastly, Jesus is the measure of your worth.

In Matthew 13, Jesus gives some very interesting examples of what the kingdom of heaven is like. In verse 44, He likens it to the man finding a treasure in a field and then selling all he had to buy the field, which we talked about near the beginning of the book. He likens it also to a pearl merchant who finds a uniquely valuable one and sells all he has to purchase it in verses 45-46.

There are stories of a similar tone in Luke 15. Jesus first talks about going to find one lost sheep, and the joy of finding it. Then He tells this story:

Or what woman, having ten silver coins, if she loses one coin, does not light a lamp, sweep the house, and search carefully until she finds it? And when she has found it, she calls her friends and neighbors together, saying, "Rejoice with me, for I have found the piece which I lost!" Likewise, I say to you, there is joy in the presence of the angels of God over one sinner who repents (verses 8-10).

I had read these scriptures many times before, but in studying Jesus for this section, I confronted myself with what it would really be like to find something so valuable that I'd be willing to sell everything I had in order to buy it. If you've never really considered it, really tried to put yourself in the shoes of someone willing to make that decision, I strongly encourage you to do so.

Selling all you own to buy something means that whatever that thing is, its worth transcends a simple dollar amount to you. It transcends any natural value that we can place on something, because for a single thing to be worth selling everything I've got, it must be pretty special. It would have to be worth it to me.

For instance, let's pretend I sold everything I own—my house and everything in it, cars, and everything else we could get our hands on—and came home and told Sarah that I had done this to buy a beautiful, Italian sports car I had seen. Remember, we are pretending. And let's say she agreed to this ridiculous idea. Obviously, still pretending.

What would we then have? We'd have a super-fast car with two seats, no food, no money to buy food, and nowhere to put it even if we did, because no one would be allowed to eat in our car. We sold everything—including our clothes—to buy the car, so now we are stuck inside the car, unable to get out. Naked.

It would not be worth it, no matter how exclusive, fast, and desirable that car was. So even though this car might be of a value equal to (or most likely greater than) everything else I own, it's not worth it to me to sell everything to buy one, because it cannot replace or improve the way we live our lives.

No matter how nice, it wouldn't be worth it to me—or you. So what would?

Some guy thought the treasure he found in this field was worth selling everything he owned. We talked about him at the beginning of the book and the no-doubt hard sell he had with his wife. "You want to sell everything we have and buy a *field?*" she would ask.

To the person who didn't know about the secret treasure, it would be foolish. They'd ask, "You sold everything for this dirt, grass, and some trees?"

But the man in Jesus' story did exactly that. He was convinced it was worth it—worth everything he owned. Perhaps that treasure would allow him to buy it all back and then some; we really don't know. But it was worth everything to him.

The same is true with the pearl merchant. He spent his days hunting for these things, and when he found an exceptional one, he sold everything he had so he could buy it. In the ancient world, pearls were considered valuable not simply because of some abstract concept of worth or rarity; they were considered some of the most beautiful things one could possess in the whole world.

It wasn't just a dollar amount that drove this guy to sell it all; it was a worth inspired by beauty that transcended simple value.

I did some study about women in the Middle East and what this coin in the last story would've meant to the woman who lost it. Young women in this area and in this era were not wealthy, generally. They would save and save, from their early teens until they got married, because they were going to wear a headdress that was very much like a wedding ring. It signified that they were married. And it was made up of ten silver coins.

Value-wise, the lost coin was worth a lot to the woman in Jesus' story. The worth of just that one coin was far greater than the literal value. To her, it was priceless—what it signified was far greater than the dollar value. So she pulled the house apart look-ing—under the couch cushions, behind the TV, in the refrigerator. Anywhere it could be, she checked. And then she checked again. And again. She's moved furniture out to the front yard, and was looking everywhere.

Then she finally found it. And when she did, she rejoiced not at the recovered value, but at the signified worth of having all of these coins, of having her symbol of something far greater than a monetary value restored.

Jesus tells us the kingdom of heaven is like that.

He tells us that we're worth paying the highest price imaginable—everything. You were worth His very life. He paid the costliest price for you.

Jesus is the measure of your worth. He set your worth as the price of His own life when He paid for you by dying. And remember, the price paid determines the value.

The Image of God

So many people don't understand the worth that Jesus set on their lives by the price He paid. They think poorly of themselves, of their worth. They see the field and think it's not worth it. They see the pearl, and they can't image why the guy paid everything for it. They see the one coin, and they don't understand why she is so excited she found it.

They don't understand the worth.

•••

THERE IS A TREASURE WITHIN YOU—
THE VERY IMAGE OF GOD.

•••

They don't understand that the hidden treasure made selling everything worth it to the guy who bought the field. They don't see the hidden treasure he saw, the deep treasure that made every penny worth spending.

They don't understand that the beauty made the pearl worth

it to the merchant. They don't see its priceless splendor the way he does.

They don't understand the significance the woman put on that one coin and what finding it restored to her. They don't know what all the celebrating is about.

They don't understand that their lives are worth so much more than the world tells them. They don't see the worth Jesus put on them, the great value He placed on each of us by willingly giving His life as the price of our redemption.

There is a treasure within you—the very image of God looking out from your eyes, walking around in your skin. The treasure within you was worth it to Him. There's a priceless beauty within you that He saw and recognized long before you were even born, before you took your first step or ever did anything, good or bad. Able to look into your heart, your hidden depths, He saw your buried treasure.

•••

JESUS CALLED YOUR WORTH—
THE SIGNIFICANCE OF A RIGHT RELATIONSHIP
BETWEEN YOU AND YOUR FATHER—
WORTH DYING FOR.

•••

You are the most beautiful thing He has ever seen and ever will see, and as an expert, He said you were worth His blood. Before you saw your first glimpse of how ugly the world is or the feeble beauty to be found here, before that colored you, He called you beautiful. And now after all you've seen and all your scars, He hasn't changed His mind—He calls you beautiful still.

Jesus called your worth—the significance of a right relationship between you and your Father—worth dying for. Long before your first individual sin, He saw you born into a fallen and sinful race; long after your final sin on this earth, He recognized that restoring you to God was worth the ultimate price. It was worth the stripes on His back, the nails in His hands and feet. You were worth the crown of thorns!

Jesus is the measure of your worth.

You meant something to Him far beyond monetary value. Just like that coin that meant something to that woman, He saw your worth. You represent something—the original plan. You represent unbroken fellowship with His creation, into whom He infused life with His breath. You represent the being He made to fellowship with, and He said Jesus was the measure of your worth—Jesus was the price worth paying for you.

What you've accomplished or what you've failed at isn't the measure; how pretty you started and the scars you've picked up aren't the measure. His blood is the measure of your worth.

That's who Jesus is. Jesus is the Word of God made flesh. Jesus is the prophetic Word fulfilled. Jesus is the most wonderful teacher, the most exciting preacher, the most gracious healer. Jesus is the measure of your wealth. He's the measure of your strength. He's the measure of your ability. Jesus is the measure of your worth.

Jesus Is: In the Bible You Own

Faith comes when you hear the Word of God, the word about Jesus. Romans 10:17 says, "Consequently, faith comes from hearing the message, and the message is heard through the word of Christ" (NIV). Another translation puts it, "So faith comes from hearing, that is, hearing the Good News about Christ" (NLT).

Faith comes when you hear about Jesus.

Why was the woman with the issue of blood so full of faith? How did the four guys and their paralyzed friend have such faith? Why was Jairus so full of faith? How were the tormented, the blind, the sick, and the lame so full of faith? Was it all the scripture they had read?

No—they heard Jesus was in town.

Faith comes by hearing about Jesus Christ, the Word made flesh, the fulfillment of prophecy, and all the rest. And we, my reader friend, have a significant advantage here: We can take hearing about Jesus and add to it the incorruptible seed of the Word of the living God that we can read every day.

Our faith is bolstered by the inspired books by Paul, Peter, James, and John—men who wrote under the direction of the Holy Spirit and gave us so much to build our faith by teaching us about Jesus. And even greater than having Him in person, we have His Word and promises sealed in His own blood. That should stir faith in anyone who will hear with an open heart, ready to receive.

That should stir you up and encourage you—you have more than just the rumors of Jesus being in town, as these people from the Gospels had. They had hope that He was what the whispers said He might be; they had heard the talk that He healed those who came to Him. And they sought Him out, did what they had to do, and in pursuing Him showed they had faith the prophecies would be fulfilled.

So we who have all the writings from then till now, who have the whole New Testament and all it teaches us about the Word made flesh, can rejoice that our faith comes by hearing about Jesus!

Jesus Is: There to Be Found

Jesus is here to be seen by any and all who will look through the eyes of faith. It simply requires a decision to open the Book. Before you sit down to read or listen to the Word of God, do something very simple first—I learned this from Sarah and it has really blessed and helped me. Before we read the Word together, she prays, "Father, we thank You for Your Word. We thank You for Jesus and the price He paid. And we thank You for the Holy Spirit, who is our guide. We believe we receive the light of revelation today as we read Your Word. Speak to us. Change us. We will be doers of the Word we hear. Amen."

•••

IF YOU WANT TO SEE HIM,
YOU ARE GOING TO HAVE TO LOOK.

•••

That simple prayer puts me in a ready position to see things I have never seen and to hear things I have never heard, even if I am reading scripture I have read a thousand times before. If you want to see Him, you are going to have to look.

Jesus Is: The Original Overcomer

A final note about confession: If you have never heard that message before, let me encourage you to study it for yourself. Our words are powerful because God's words are powerful.

Jesus Himself said that we could have the things we say. So it's important to ask yourself, are you speaking words of life or death? How often do you hear yourself say things like "I can't do," or "I can't have" or "This is killing me"? These are words that we cannot allow in our vocabulary.

Our words are far more serious than you may have at first realized. Let me remind you of how you were born again: You believed that Jesus is the Son of God, then you *said* it. The Bible tells us that with the heart man believes unto righteousness; with the mouth, confession is made unto salvation. In other words, it is by believing in your heart that you are made right with God, and it is by confessing with your mouth that you are saved (Romans 10:10).

If your words are powerful enough to change eternity, they can certainly have an effect on the world we live in today. Make sure your words line up with His Words.

You are an overcomer. Say it. "I am an overcomer." Now make it a complete and powerful confession: "I am an overcomer *through Him who loves me.*"

•••

> IF YOUR WORDS ARE POWERFUL ENOUGH TO CHANGE ETERNITY, THEY CAN CERTAINLY HAVE AN AFFECT ON THE WORLD WE LIVE IN TODAY.

•••

Who Do You Say Jesus Is?

At the beginning of this book, I told you that we would answer Jesus' question, "Who do you say that I am?"

I say that He is the Christ, the Son of the Living God. I say that He is my Savior, my Healer, my Guide, and my Brother. He is first place in my life above any other. He is my love, and I am His.

This book is who I say He is because it is what I have found His Word to say about Him. That is the way I fill in the blank.

Now you fill it in. God is _____.

Who do you say that He is?

Appendix

HEALING SCRIPTURES

Exodus 15:26

If you diligently heed the voice of the Lord your God and do what is right in His sight, give ear to His commandments and keep all His statutes, I will put none of the diseases on you which I have brought on the Egyptians. For I am the Lord who heals you.

Exodus 23:25-26

So you shall serve the Lord your God, and He will bless your bread and your water. And I will take sickness away from the midst of you. No one shall suffer miscarriage or be barren in your land; I will fulfill the number of your days.

Psalm 103:2-3

Bless the Lord, O my soul, and forget not all His benefits: who forgives all your iniquities, who heals all your diseases.

Psalm 105:37

He also brought them out with silver and gold, and there was none feeble among His tribes.

Psalm 107:20

He sent His word and healed them, and delivered them from their destructions.

Isaiah 53:4-5

Surely He has borne our griefs and carried our sorrows; yet we esteemed Him stricken, smitten by God, and afflicted. But He was wounded for our transgressions, He was bruised for our iniquities; the chastisement for our peace was upon Him, and by His stripes we are healed.

Isaiah 58:8

Then your light shall break forth like the morning, your healing shall spring forth speedily, and your righteousness shall go before you; the glory of the Lord shall be your rear guard.

Malachi 4:2

But to you who fear My name the Sun of Righteousness shall arise with healing in His wings; and you shall go out and grow fat like stall-fed calves.

Matthew 8:16-17

When evening had come, they brought to Him many who were demon-possessed. And He cast out the spirits with a word, and healed all who were sick, that it might be fulfilled which was spoken by Isaiah the prophet, saying: "He Himself took our infirmities and bore our sicknesses."

Matthew 9:35

Then Jesus went about all the cities and villages, teaching in their synagogues, preaching the gospel of the kingdom, and healing every sickness and every disease among the people.

Matthew 10:1

And when He had called His twelve disciples to Him, He gave them power over unclean spirits, to cast them out, and to heal all kinds of sickness and all kinds of disease.

Mark 11:22-24

So Jesus answered and said to them, "Have faith in God. For assuredly, I say to you, whoever says to this mountain, 'Be removed and be cast into the sea,' and does not doubt in his heart, but believes that those things he says will be done, he will have whatever he says. Therefore I say to you, whatever things you ask when you pray, believe that you receive them, and you will have them."

Mark 16:17-18

And these signs will follow those who believe: In My name they will cast out demons; they will speak with new tongues; they will take up serpents; and if they drink anything deadly, it will by no means hurt them; they will lay hands on the sick, and they will recover.

Acts 3:16

And His name, through faith in His name, has made this man strong, whom you see and know. Yes, the faith which comes through Him has given him this perfect soundness in the presence of you all.

Acts 10:38

How God anointed Jesus of Nazareth with the Holy Spirit and with power, who went about doing good and healing all who were oppressed by the devil, for God was with Him.

Romans 8:11

But if the Spirit of Him who raised Jesus from the dead dwells in you, He who raised Christ from the dead will also give life to your mortal bodies through His Spirit who dwells in you.

James 5:14-16

Is anyone among you sick? Let him call for the elders of the church, and let them pray over him, anointing him with oil in the name of the Lord. And the prayer of faith will save the sick, and the Lord will raise him up. And if he has committed sins, he will be forgiven. Confess your trespasses to one another, and pray for one another, that you may be healed. The effective, fervent prayer of a righteous man avails much.

1 Peter 2:24

Who Himself bore our sins in His own body on the tree, that we, having died to sins, might live for righteousness— by whose stripes you were healed.

3 John 2

Beloved, I pray that you may prosper in all things and be in health, just as your soul prospers.

Prayer of Salvation

God is a loving Father who knows you better than you know yourself. Now He wants you to know Him in the same personal way. The first and most important step in this is to make Jesus first place in your life. Just pray this simple prayer aloud:

Heavenly Father, I am coming to You now in the Name of Your Son Jesus. I believe with all my heart that He is the Savior of the world. I believe He lived, died and rose from the dead, and that He did it all for me. I ask You to cleanse me of all my sin. Wash me clean and make me new. Thank You for the gift that You gave me in Jesus. I receive Him now as my Lord. Fill me with Your Holy Spirit. I receive His help, courage and strength to live a victorious life. I am Yours forever. In Jesus' Name. Amen.

About the Author

Jeremy Pearsons is a third-generation minister who has spent his life in and around worldwide ministry. He and his wife, Sarah, minister out of their desire to see people from all walks of life come to know the life-changing power of Jesus Christ, the Living Word of God. They minister to congregations in their hometown of Fort Worth, Texas, and around the world. Jeremy and Sarah teach believers of all ages to hold fast to the same spirit of faith as those who have gone before, and to reach behind to those who will follow.

"There are two kinds of legacies: the one you keep and the one you leave."

For more information about this book and other resource materials, go to www.jeremypearsons.com.

Sarah Hart Pearsons

Love Songs for the King

Love Songs for the King is the debut worship album from Sarah Hart Pearsons. This project features 12 original songs that will ignite the heart of worship within you. For more information or to purchase your copy please visit www.sarahhartpearsons.com.